T0317780

"The best seller from Italy". Scavolini 1961–2011

"The best seller from Italy"
Scavolini 1961–2011

50 Years of Kitchens

edited by Massimo Martignoni

SKIRA

Art Director
Marcello Francone

Design
Luigi Fiore

Editorial Coordination
Vincenza Russo

Editing
Timothy Stroud

Layout
Serena Parini

Translations
Jeff Jennings for Language Consulting
Congressi, Milan

Photography Credits
Gabriele Basilico
Filippo Romano
Archivio Scavolini Spa,
unless otherwise indicated

Acknowledgements
Adi, Associazione per il Disegno
industriale, Milano
Elena Rosa Caputo
Cosmit spa, Milano
Christopher Dougherty
Ferruccio Luppi
Fondazione Piero Portaluppi, Milano
Patrizia Malfatti

FC Media Service
Komma
Studio Roscio
Studio 33

First published in Italy in 2010 by
Skira Editore S.p.A.
Palazzo Casati Stampa
via Torino 61
20123 Milano
Italy
www.skira.net

Printed and bound in Italy. First edition

Distributed in North America by Rizzoli
International Publications, Inc., 300 Park
Avenue South, New York, NY 10010,
USA.
Distributed elsewhere in the world by
Thames and Hudson Ltd., 181A High
Holborn, London WC1V 7QX, United
Kingdom.

Contents

Choose a job you love, and you will never
have to work a day in your life
Confucius

Foreword

This book recounts the first fifty years of the history of Scavolini, starting from what now seems like long ago and arriving well past the threshold of the new millennium. A lot has happened in this half-century. Scavolini has grown and established itself as "the best seller from Italy", expanding to an international scale. But we at Scavolini haven't changed. We're the same as ever—a group that continues to believe in the values of work and collective commitment, with respect for each other and our surroundings, in the idea that it's not only possible but a duty to improve what has already been accomplished. Our group consists of 660 people who work side-by-side every day. It may sound trite to say that we're like a big family, but it's also not far from the truth: a family composed of all those who have worked with us and since retired or are no longer with us; a family that extends to our close-knit network of suppliers, dealers, agents and outside collaborators, in Italy and abroad. I hope that in these few lines I have captured the value and the uniqueness of our splendid group spirit and, if I could, I would thank all the people, one by one, who have traveled with us on this great adventure.

Valter Scavolini
November 2010

Introduction

Philippe Daverio

Fernand Braudel is unquestionably the historian who, better than any other, has dissected the intricate mechanisms that have driven Mediterranean culture for three millennia. There's just one aspect of his sublime reasoning that might be subject to question, and that is the role and meaning of the kitchen. The volume that made him famous, entitled *The Mediterranean and the Mediterranean World in the Era of Philip II* (1949), is a sort of grammar of civilization, wherein more and less important information is interwoven with interpretations of political and cultural history, all in three volumes that changed the history of studying history in the West. In the 1980s, toward the end of his long life as a scholar, he published a brief and accessible treatise collecting his own writings and those of his collaborators that ingeniously and perspicaciously summarized his thoughts, entitled simply, *The Mediterranean*. It is there that he posits a highly intriguing thesis on the difference between the populations of Northern Europe, who tend to gather around the hearth, and those of the Mediterranean, for whom the heart of the home is 'Penelope's loom', i.e. the mother. This analysis, however acute, is not entirely applicable to Italy, not even the proto-Italy of ancient times. Because here, even as early as the Roman era, the home was already a complex space, full of differentiated zones to the point that it really becomes impossible to know where, physically, the true center was. But one thing is absolutely certain: by comparison to the huts of the barbarian cultures, our ancestors saw the kitchen as far more complex than simply the site of the hearth. The Villa of Poppea in the Oplontis site just outside of Pompeii, one of the most beautiful Roman villas of the first century, whose structure and decorations remain mostly intact, is probably where the empress (the wife of Emperor Nero) died when Vesuvius erupted in 79 AD. The house is typical: salons, ceremonial decorations and faux stuccos, patios and porticoes...but most significantly for our purposes, a vast kitchen decorated with frescoes and encaustic panels that suggest the ease with which the empress must have circulated among her cooks as they worked. The Versailles of Louis XIV, sixteen centuries later, has a kitchen that resembles a factory, entirely devoid of the grace of the Roman kitchen. And this is easily explained: the Roman dwelling was not conceived for courtiers but for *gens*, a vast and articulated nuclear family where the matron ruled with the same determination with which she sought to tame the whims of Nero. The Italian kitchen has always been a convivial place, never merely the room where food is cooked. The Italian kitchen combines the power of Penelope and the hearth, in a space designed to accommodate both the passage of the poet and the creative appetites of Trimalchio. Obviously it has evolved since then, changing in step with shifting customs and the shrinking family unit. But its first, original raison d'être has never been lost.

The Baroque period was characterized by a spreading of the wealth beyond the previous limits of royal privilege and across a wider social sphere to which many had access. The villa, even the castle, began to appear all over Europe, and urban *palazzi* multiplied like loaves and fishes. The quantity of painting produced grew proportionally. Genres designed solely for pleasure were born, foremost among which was the still-life. But the destiny of canvases was quite different. In puritanical, bourgeois Holland, the still-life was hung in the dining room and featured prized foods on silver trays surrounded by precious glassware. In the homes of the nobility, it depicted instead the fruits of the hunt, where hares and venison stood as proof of class privilege, insofar as the same game had it been hunted by a simple farmer would have earned him a criminal indictment. The rooms of the prelates and the salons of the potentates were filled instead with compositions of flowers and fruit which, while sometimes charged with symbolism, were invariably intended to signify luxury. Only in Italy did an absolutely unique phenomenon develop: paintings, both small and enormous, made specifically for the kitchen. Already by the end of the sixteenth century, the Campi brothers were painting still-lifes of butchered meat. Then came the kitchen scenes of Baschenis and dell'Empoli, with dozens of chickens and ducks prepared for cooking. From Emilia to Naples, paintings were commissioned for the kitchen, and certainly not for the visual enjoyment of the cooking staff, not even for that of the imported French chefs whom the Neapolitans called *monsù*. Because, while the cooks flipped their pans and stirred their sauces, the masters of the house came to watch, whetting their appetites while contemplating the filleted fish painted by Levoli, or those arranged among branches of coral by Recco. The kitchen was a necessary and integral part of domestic life.

In this year of the 150th anniversary of the Unification of Italy, a great number of paintings of the sort usually forgotten in the darkened hallways of private collections or in the basements of history museums are being dusted off, some of which are genuine masterpieces of the nineteenth century. Perhaps the most engaging and interesting documents from that era are the works of the soldier/painter Gerolamo Induno. Although, owing to inclination and personal history, he painted mostly battle scenes, he did not hesitate to apply his grittily realistic narration to scenes of what went on behind those battles, that is, among the families of the soldiers: the letter that arrives from the front and is read by the father, an authoritative gentleman with a silver-handled walking stick, surrounded by his family in their Brianza villa; the story recounted by the wounded soldier to a young girl, who looks at him with apparent modesty that fails to conceal her passion. All of this takes place in homes that are anything but poor, but where the parsimony and frugality of bourgeois respectability do not necessarily manifest themselves in fresh maintenance. Everything happens in the kitchen, by a hearth in which a small cooking fire perennially burns. The walls are laden with domestic utensils that would make an antique dealer drool; tables from earlier centuries are conserved with the same care that has kept the villa itself standing for centuries. But always in the kitchen....

While Europe was getting back on its feet after World War II, while the French were refurbishing their salons and the Germans were putting their goose-down duvets back on their beds, the Italians dedicated themselves to remodeling the kitchen. A genetic mutation occurred, a cross-breeding of species. For thousands of years, the rich man's kitchen and the poor man's hearth coexisted. The hearth enjoyed great cinematic fortune through the movies of Neo-Realism directors, generating a sub-genre within genre films: the dinner scene, the eternal archetype of the family gathered around the table, discussing politics while the pasta is being drained. The sink crouches coyly in the corner, while the entire scene takes place beneath a single lamp, on a plastic tablecloth, in front of the credenza that closes the wall of the low-cost kitchen. The nobler model was instead slowly fading, along with the disappearance of maidservants and an extended domestic service: the kitchen, on the other hand, that had elevated its status to include the pantry in truth was only worthy of country villas or full-floor city apartments. Reality was undergoing a revolution and homes everywhere were becoming more contained. The hearth of small "courtyard" houses found itself mixed by necessity with the noble kitchen. A dangerous hybrid could have developed from this; indeed, there were cases of frightening genetic mutations still visible today in certain small dining-rooms, in certain mysterious cellars, in the difficulty of sliding into the built-in bench that surrounds the table like a horseshoe. As fate would have it, the Americans won the war and America saved Italy from further perversion of the kitchen. The smiling consumerism of the 1950s taught us the supreme virtue of the mono-block, modular kitchen, which called first and foremost for a dialogue with the refrigerator and brought with it the washing machine as a natural evolution and the dishwasher as the feminine dream of redemption. It was depicted in dozens of films as a possible consequence of a new social code, where the family had dinner by candlelight in the dining room, but found its true cohesion over a breakfast of coffee and muffins, the father leafing through the newspaper before grabbing his briefcase and driving to the office, the mother affectionately conveying the day's instructions to the children as they go off to school, leaving her alone in the house to wait for the postman. This model of life was not really applicable in Italy, where breakfast means an espresso at the bar, or a brioche and cappuccino, so neither was that typology of kitchen. But the three instances mixed together the popular, the elite and the American and, almost like the boom of that period, the Italian miracle was born. This model corresponded to the kitchen designed and built in a flexible and therefore universal way: it was the true democratic conquest of the country, the acquisition of a transversal privilege that objectively found, in 1961, year of the centennial of Italian Unification, its date of confirmation. It is only by following this route, sometimes with a dutifully generous and ironic eye, that one can explain the industrial evolution of a sector that was and still is a driving force in the overall economy. The field of furniture production, including the 'high design' furniture that today has expanded forcefully beyond its niche, experienced the transformation in 60 years from the artisanal to the industrial in almost all of its sectors. However, this industrial transformation deserves a further explanation: manual ability has by no means disappeared, and if one thinks in the industrial sense, it is certainly not in the Fordist key. Industry means design, planning, promotion, replicable professionalism, mechanical production; but it doesn't necessarily mean vast nuclei of manual labor. Many companies, even the most brilliant, are not very large. With the exception of those that make kitchens: the kitchen generated the factory, a human factory where all the skill of the artisans of yesteryear remain. And the reason is very simple, tied naturally to the dimension of a market that has always represented the most expensive of all home furnishing components for families Italian families, that is, which have always imagined the kitchen as a human factory, a gathering place where a high degree of artisanal skill reigns.

This is why it came almost automatically to Scavolini to choose this family as the interface with its customers, back in the days before marketing surveys ruled and things were left to the intuition of the businessman. This is the reason for the choice of spokeswomen like Carrà and Cuccarini, who perfectly represented the identity of the nuclear family of the time, daily penetrating that same nuclear family through the television screen, thus becoming a direct, first-person relationship.

Scavolini developed in the kitchen sector almost with naturalness. The practice of the organization enabled them to devise a rational approach to product standardization while keeping the original commitment to quality alive and immediately conducting the company into the world of design, which was then shaping the new Italian taste.

On the Adriatic coast, companies have grown on the basis of a social cohesion that served as fertile soil. But there was also a tradition which, in the kitchen and in the female figure that sustained and governed it, the famous *resdora*, had already creatively combined the function of the hearth with that of the kitchen as the power station of everyday domestic life. Federico Fellini affectionately recounted this very tradition in *Amarcord*. All Scavolini had to do was make the leap into modernity, and the adventure was underway....

Gabriele Basilico

Montelabbate, Pesaro June 2010

28

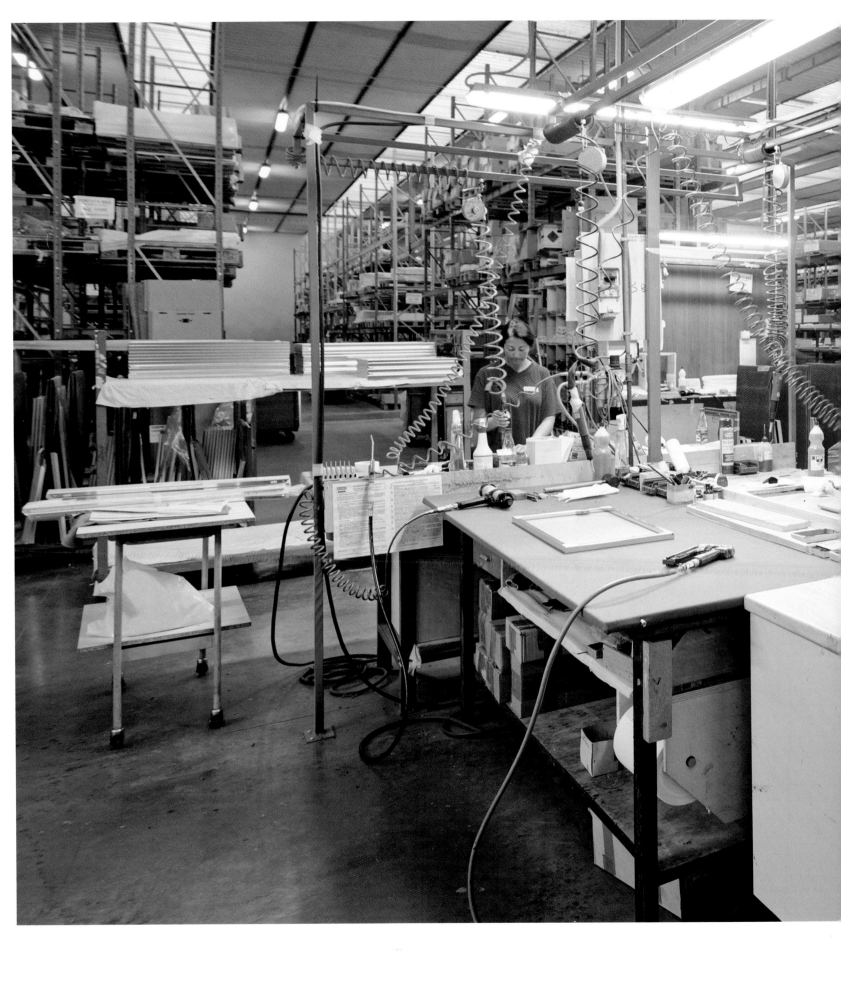

Massimo Martignoni

Scavolini 1961–2011

Tetrix (Michael Young,
2011) embodies
Scavolini's attention
to new ideas in
contemporary design

The Scavolini Formula

This book celebrates an important landmark for a company that epitomizes the 'Made in Italy' ethos. In a crowded market sector like that of the industrially-produced modular kitchen, the name Scavolini has earned the trust of millions of people over the years and has become internationally synonymous with Italian quality and taste.

The Group's numbers are solid: a logistical headquarters on the outskirts of Pesaro of 2,800,000 square feet (1,240,000 indoors), more than 650 employees, annual revenues of over 280 million dollars, a turnover that has a significant impact on the local economy through the business it provides to suppliers of components, a current range of 65 base models in 340 finishes and thousands of variations. Half a century seems more than enough to justify taking a backwards look at the history of a company that has crossed the threshold from being a successful manufacturing outfit to a cultural force in shaping our domestic landscape and customs.

However, we need to start from today to follow the path of Scavolini, a name and brand inextricably bound to the talent and entrepreneurial intelligence of its founder, Valter Scavolini, who launched the company in 1961, and his brother Elvino, Valter's inseparable alter ego, who joined the company a few years later and remained until his death in 2004. Forthright, austere and, in the best Italian tradition, proud of his upbringing in the religion of hard work, Valter Scavolini is a true captain of industry. "A company is a machine that must always be kept in perfect working order"[1] is one of his mantras, somewhere between Enzo Ferrari and Le Corbusier. He is a man who never stops to linger on the glories of the past, and this is why his manufacturing model continues to stand up to the challenges of contemporary industry. Born during the Italian economic boom, Scavolini kitchens managed to conquer a specific corner of the market by

focusing on high quality and affordability, a tempered response to stylistic values (which, when considered as a whole, provide direct evidence of the changes in taste over the past half century), and a clear message of practicality and everyday usage.

These are kitchens designed to convey the Italian sense of domestic conviviality: not abstract Modernist set designs, but spaces where real people get together to prepare real food and enjoy it together. This is how Scavolini has always conceived its kitchens. It was true then, and is perhaps even truer today, following the rediscovery of the cultural and psychological benefits that result from the daily ritual of cooking.

The Scavolini kitchens of today thus have solid roots in the formula that has been the main reason for its success from the outset: a rational vision of the supply chain designed to continuously optimize the production process, from planning to assembly to distribution, which provides a signal of implicit

quality to the customer. Thanks in part to a shrewd use of advertising (television and otherwise, with regard to which Scavolini has always shown uncommon far-sightedness) and to a trusted network of dealers, customers know that their kitchen is the result of a process marked by excellence, and that the price is fair.

"Designing and building beautiful, reliable, safe and environmentally respectful kitchens that totally satisfy the needs of our customers" is one of the central aims of the Scavolini philosophy, as are "keeping costs at competitive levels; guaranteeing high standards of product and service quality; always delivering on time; constantly improving all company processes and monitoring them efficiently; raising our suppliers' awareness of the issues of quality, ecology, and the importance of health and safety in the workplace." The list goes on: "Improving internal and external communication; controlling and reducing the consumption of

Atelier (Studio Vuesse, 2010) brings to life the idea of the practical, functional kitchen that has always been a guiding principle for Scavolini

resources; controlling and reducing emissions and waste; lowering health and safety risks for workers; making innovation affordable by improving all processes; rigorously respecting all applicable laws and norms; emphasizing human and moral values on both the business and production sides; respecting the environment in every phase of our activity."[2] It is through these principles, the direct expression of Scavolini's modus operandi, that the brand has gradually distinguished itself from its competitors. The Scavolini formula is as effective as it is simple: always look ahead without ever forgetting where you came from.

Scavolini Today

Alongside a wide range of models and custom options, the Scavolini kitchens of the new millennium highlight the growing role of the individual designer. Perry King and Santiago Miranda, Karim Rashid, Michael Young, as well as Giugiaro Design and other Italian designers[3] are the names that appear in the impeccable settings and photography of the company's catalogs. The settings, be they metropolitan glamour or immersed in nature, are elegant yet without that glacial detachment that one often encounters in the iconography of high-end kitchens. If a glass of red wine should be spilled on a table, or a ripe tomato fall on the floor, it's not the end of the world, say these images. Because these spaces, while beautiful and perfectly arranged, still maintain the aspect of being used by real people: creative professionals with lots of friends, young couples with or without children, relaxed contemporary families. The message conveyed is the pleasure of domestic intimacy, the idea of happiness as a temporary but tangible state that the

Scenery (Perry King,
Santiago Miranda, 2008),
the kitchen as theatrical
stage, the visual fulcrum
of the home of the new
millennium

The harmony of forms
and proportions of Crystal
(Studio Vuesse, 2004)

ritual of cooking and dining together
enables us to achieve. This is the same
message of Scavolini ads in the past.
The only significant difference today is
that the tone of both the products and
communications has become more sober
and almost minimal.

What started out at the end of the last
century as a reaction against the
unfettered decorative dimension of the
1980s, a revival of the eternally valid
slogan "Less is more", has since become
a widely accepted rule. Though it is not
ever possible to entirely exclude the
possibility of a return to a baroque
sensibility, the notions of beauty and
comfort have evolved over the past two
decades. Minimalism has become an
aesthetic code that calls for subtraction
rather than addition, the simplification
of forms and volumes, and the reduction
or indeed elimination of all
ornamentation. It's what works now.
A sophisticated interpretation of this
code is the Tetrix kitchen by Michael
Young,[4] one of the latest from Scavolini,
due to its synthesis of the image and
philosophy of the brand through the use
of new parameters, both in the

conceptual terms of its aesthetics and in
the functional terms that explicitly
announce its ease and immediacy of
use. Previewed in Milan at Eurocucina
2010,[5] Tetrix is an intelligent reflection
on the inexhaustible theme of
modularity, so deeply bound to the
history of kitchen design as to
constitute its main guiding principle.
Focusing on the tenet that governs the
mechanics of the alignments, which are
no longer fixed and immutable, Young
has conceived a system of free and
articulated additions which do not,
however, compromise the elegant
sobriety of the whole. This is a project
that deftly encapsulates the experience
accumulated by Scavolini during its
first 50 years while at the same time
pointing towards intriguing new
prospects for future developments.[6]
Whether it is the clean geometry of
Michael Young's designs, the reliable
technological vision of Giugiaro Design
or the aesthetically graphic approach of
Karim Rashid, the 'designer model'
targets the values of a certain type of
clientele, mostly young and up-to-date,
who wish to keep pace with the lexical

developments in contemporary design. This is the audience that Rashid himself addresses, on camera, when describing his approach to kitchen design. "Scavolini is a company I had always dreamed of working with," he recounts. "The quality of their work is just fantastic. So I was quite surprised when they knocked on my door and asked me to work on the Crystal collection, or rather to decorate or interpret it through my spirit, my aesthetic. Scavolini kitchens have a very modern line, with clean, regular geometry. When I saw their designs I thought that we really have reached the point where the kitchen has become a very, very refined object. So my idea was to add a bit of my Pop, or 'post-Pop' spirit. Today the kitchen space represents the place where the transmission of different levels of energy and inspiration is most apparent, and this is because two aspects coexist there: one is social life, parties and such—at parties you can see how many guests end up staying in the kitchen all night—and the other is obviously cooking. When preparing food, you need inspiration, and in my view there's nothing better for inspiration than increasing the power, the beauty, the aesthetics, the color and surfaces and textures of a kitchen. So I took some pattern designs I work with and adapted them to the Crystal collection, also working on the fixtures and exhaust hood to create a truly alternative effect, something more colorful and lively. Why? Because I'm inspired by life itself."[7]

The fact that Karim Rashid has in a sense 'dressed' one of the company's flagship models with his flamboyant personality is indicative. The public that appreciates the digital decorations of the eclectic designer does not have to miss out on the spirit of Italian design—i.e., harmony of rhythms and dimensions, attention to detail, absence of vulgar or aggressive juxtapositions—of which Scavolini is by its very nature a proud standard-bearer. There are many different factors that determine the path of a company for which, for numerous reasons, the combination of tradition and innovation is essential. The way that Scavolini looks toward the future without forgetting its origins, the way the company projects itself forward without leaving its vast treasury of experience behind—these are indicative both of business acumen and mental flexibility.

"To reap, one must sow, even when things are going well. One must always invest and experiment. Especially now that competition has gone global," Valter Scavolini declares.[8] This is why, along with playing the contemporary design card, which is *de rigueur* for competing in certain areas of the home furnishing industry, the company's policy also includes kitchens that satisfy the expectations of customers less inclined toward the new and anchored to the idea of the traditional kitchen, which still manages to survive despite everything. It is not a contradiction, therefore, to find the aforementioned models alongside kitchens that give a nod to the timeless memory of the past through a new interpretation of classic designs. A clever strategy aware of the preference for these typologies in certain geographical areas and/or specific strata of the population uses the fascination with the memory of yesteryear as the guiding thread for a series of kitchens designed by Gianni Pareschi, Marco Pareschi and Raffaello Pravato.

In particular, the Absolute Classic range, according to its creator Gianni Pareschi, "speaks a language that exists outside of time and fashion" and seeks to restore dignity to stylistic elements belonging from a traditional

The Scavolini stand
at exhibitions in 2010:
at the KBB fair in
Birmingham (left) and
Eurocucina in Milan (right)

In-house postcard, 2010

background that have been "for too long banished by official culture". Pareschi continues, "designing for Scavolini means knowing how to work outside the dictates of design. Scavolini has an all-round approach, and this means acknowledging the dignity and validity of all its customers' tastes, different as they may be. Not everyone likes nouvelle cuisine, and in the same way not everyone wants to live in a kitchen that feels like an art gallery—which is what the dominant aesthetic of contemporary design sometimes suggests—where there's plenty of rigor, sure, but where some people feel uneasy about actually cooking there. What Scavolini asks from the designer is to understand how to interpret the dreams of very different customers. It is from this challenge that Absolute Classic was born, an 'absolute' response to those looking for classic style in a high-end kitchen."[9]

The New Italian and International Scene

In light of what we have examined thus far, the characteristics of Scavolini products and the company itself appear to be a direct consequence of an evolutionary process at once cultural, industrial and managerial, one that has developed in tandem with the company's growth in the Italian market and, since the late 1980s, in the global market as well. From the beginning, this development was never one-way; it was never a mechanical expansion of Scavolini know-how across the country. Instead it has progressed by relying on its network of suppliers and dealers. It would not be wrong, then, to identify this as one of the crucial strengths of the company's strategy. "It was our suppliers, all Italian, who enabled us years ago to move up to the next level," recalls Valter Scavolini. "Without them, without decentralizing production, we would never have been able to grow as we did. That really was a very far-sighted decision."[10]

Similarly important is the attention given to every dealership in the sales network, due to the importance of their strategic role, the skills of the dealers themselves, and their relevance to the demand for innovation that the market constantly poses. "For Scavolini, the dealer plays a crucial role as it is at the point of sale that the customer and manufacturer 'meet'. It's up to the dealer to correctly interpret the expectations of the customer and satisfy his needs using the solutions we have provided. Scavolini assists the dealer in everything, never leaving him on his

Scavolini Soho Gallery, the company's flagship store in Manhattan, November 2010

own and facilitating his job in every way."[11] To manage communication with its network and be able to intervene in real time, Scavolini uses a system of professional management and updating tools.[12]

From the first points of sale in central Italy, where Scavolini enjoyed its earliest commercial success, to today, expansion has been rapid and continuous. The foundation of the system is a network in Italy of more than 1000 stores. The company's steady march across the globe began in Greece when the first foreign outlet was opened in 1987. Now there is a worldwide network of about 300 showrooms in more than 50 countries on 5 continents.[13] An important recent aspect of this process is Scavolini Stores, a strategic operation aimed at further strengthening the brand's identity. The Stores are specialized kitchen centers dedicated exclusively to Scavolini products. Since 2006, approximately 100 have been opened in large Italian and foreign cities. "With this formula, the company is not attempting to replace the existing distribution network, but operate alongside and support it. This choice has led to an increase in revenues in the relevant areas, which can be attributed in part to the brand's increased visibility."[14]

Scavolini is now entering a new phase. Its stable presence in the leading countries in Europe and numerous key areas of the world—from the Middle East, India and China to the United States, Latin America and Oceania—has greatly reinforced the international perception of the company as being synonymous with Italian design and taste, a phenomenon that is supported by Scavolini's regular presence at important trade shows (Basel, Birmingham, Brussels, Chicago, Dubai, Moscow, Mumbai, Paris, Toronto). While this attests to the company's

success, it brings with it certain obligations—the greater the exposure, the greater the responsibility. The new stores expand the distribution network and, at the same time, increase the importance of a program that exports, along with kitchens, a specific cultural message associated with the brand's Italian roots.

This is the thread that has underlain all the recent openings and future plans for expansion—from Belgium, where a new store opened in September 2009 in Antwerp's fashionable 't Zuid district, to India, site of an intensive program already underway in Hyderabad, Bangalore and Chennai, with stores opening soon in New Delhi, Mumbai and Pune; from Southeast Asia, with openings in Singapore and Bangkok to join the existing Scavolini Stores in Taipei and Shanghai, to South and Central America, with upcoming openings in Lima, Santiago del Chile, Guatemala City, Panama and many other locations. The growing number of mono-brand stores in African countries—Nigeria, Angola, Kenya, Morocco and Libya—is indicative of a new focus on a continent with enormous growth potential. Another new frontier is the United States, for which a specific program has been devised, starting with the creation of Scavolini USA, Inc., and the acquisition of a former art gallery of nearly 8,400 square feet on West Broadway in SoHo, New York, the first true flagship store on American soil, which represents a significant acceleration in the growth of an already formidable sales network. This has been a brief summary of just a few of the more recent steps that shed light on Scavolini's steady expansion, clear signals of entrepreneurial courage in a period when the global economy is in great difficulty. But history teaches that the best moment to charge forward is when the road goes uphill.

Flux (Giugiaro Design, 2007) is the expression of a new approach to design while respecting the values of Scavolini

Tribe (Marcello Cutino,
2009), an interpretation
of the contemporary
that breaks free of the
minimalist canon

Baccarat (Gianni
Pareschi, 2006),
a contemporary take
on tradition

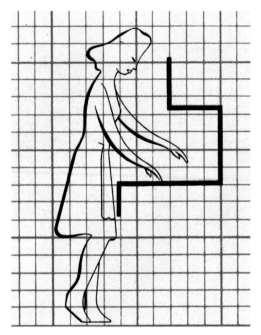

The drive toward the standardization of dimensions and components was the focus of kitchen design after the Second World War
Above
L'Architecture d'Aujourd'Hui, March 1947

Below
From left, *Intérieur*, March 1958; *House & Garden*, July 1951

Opposite
Meanwhile, European architects of the 1920s and '30s were still bound to the idea of the traditional kitchen. Interior by Josef Hoffmann, from *Speisezimmer und Küchen*, Alexander Koch, Darmstadt 1921

Scavolini's Place in the History of Kitchen Design

Fifty years of production and a portfolio of 150 different models. Scandinavian echoes of the company's first kitchens and the progressive 'Italianization' of the models of the 1960s. Partnerships with designers and the revival of traditional materials and decoration in the '70s. The postmodernism and dramatic flair of the '80s. The kitchen-laboratory of the '90s and the extreme customization and technological sophistication of today. To browse the pages of Scavolini's catalogue is to retrace the evolution of the kitchen in the context of the modern domestic landscape. The sequence provides a realistic snapshot of the history of recent social customs. By virtue of the company's firmly established image, multiple connections are revealed of the public's real-life experience in the home, from the shifting tastes of 'normal' people (which are far more indicative of an epoch than those of the elite) to the social and cultural changes that take place in family life. It is worth noting that Scavolini's development took place within the borders of the country in which it was born long before extending to foreign horizons. This is why it might be useful, and in a certain sense necessary for documentary purposes, to examine some of the salient points in the evolution of kitchen design, prioritizing the Italian point of view. Looking back, the transformation of the kitchen since the Second World War seems surprising. Fifty years ago, the unquestioned paradigm was the American kitchen, either in direct form or imitated by European manufacturers. Today, the Italian kitchen has become the paradigm around the world, and the many reasons for this success can be boiled down to two key points: on one hand, the increasing success of the Italian furniture industry, in which the kitchen has been one of its main strengths since the 1960s; on the other hand, the

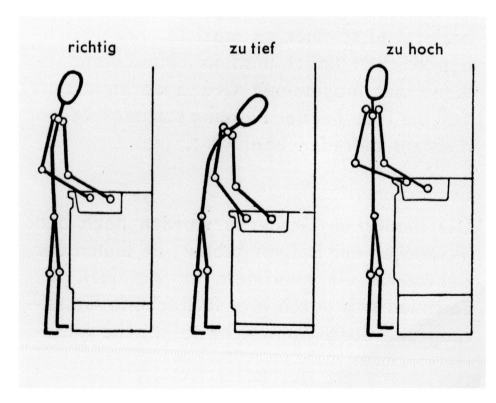

growing conviction worldwide that the Italian way of life corresponds to a standard of exemplary quality, particularly with regard to one of its most distinguishing features—the everyday preparation of food.

The ritual of cooking in Italy is one expression of a complex and multi-layered culture, which contains in its DNA the principle of handing down through the generations of rules and recipes that are often many hundreds of years old. This process has been very important historically, as it keeps alive an archive of tastes unique in the world and constitutes one of the few recognizable pillars of a collective identity in Italy.[15] Yet it has also been restrictive in other ways, most of all because of its aversion to codification. This is made all the clearer when Italy is compared with France, which is far more careful about officializing recipes, cooking techniques, cheese production and winemaking. As often happens in Italy, genius and intemperance go hand in hand, and cooking is no exception. "Ignore books that address this art: they are mostly either wrong or incomprehensible, particularly the Italian ones, a bit less so the French." These are the words of Pellegrino Artusi, who presumed he could do better, as they are taken from the introduction to his famous cookbook of 1891.[16]

The general reluctance to constrain the ancient, almost innate culinary knowledge of Italy is responsible for the delay in the introduction of technological innovation to the Italian domestic environment. The times and rhythms of cooking, even well into the twentieth century, were still governed by an organization of work that was often and deliberately irrational, sometimes even archaic. This was because the time a woman spent in the kitchen, stirring sauces for hours and hours, was perceived as tangible proof of the solidity of family values, and therefore not to be meddled with. Echoes of this fundamental contradiction—such as a noble and widespread gastronomic culture, and strong resistance (at least until the 1960s) to changing deeply-rooted habits—are apparent in the world of design that we are about to investigate.

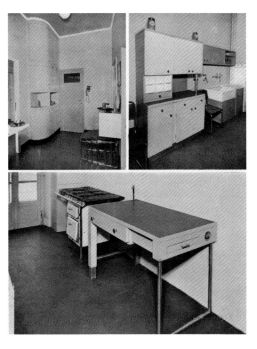

When Architects Discovered the Kitchen

"The cook's galley on a steamship has every article and utensil used in cooking for two hundred persons in a space not larger than the stove room, and so arranged that with one or two steps the cook can reach all he uses. In contrast to this, in most large houses, the table furniture, the cooking materials and utensils, the sink and the eating room are at such distances apart that half the time and strength is employed in walking back and forth to collect and return the articles used." Thus wrote Catharine E. Beecher in her *American Woman's Home* of 1869, a manual of home economics co-written with her sister, Harriet Beecher Stowe,[17] wherein she presents a series of suggestions for a new distribution of kitchen space based on the rational use of compact, shelved spaces that are a surprising anticipation of the *Frankfurter Küche* designed by Margarete Schütte-Lihotzky more than 50 years later. The space described in the *Nomenclatura domestica italiana* by Agostino Fecia, published just after Beecher's book, seems to belong to an entirely different epoch judging by the organizational anarchy that distinguishes it: "the kitchen, although underground, is well-lit for it is illuminated from on high by open windows with deep embrasures in the walls on the sides and below: it is furnished with everything that serves for cooking, its fireplace is of the ancient type and thus very spacious; the hearth is fitted with large boards, the opposite wall looking upon the activities of the fireplace from a large pediment…".[18] And so forth, with a myriad of objects positioned here and there—"quivers, hooks and ramps…the box for salt and spices, the pepper pot, and in the middle the coffee pot and chocolate pan, and

along with them whisks, vases and jars of various dimensions, skewers, spits, spikes and other utensils for roasting"—without any apparent order. This is why Valter Scavolini likes to joke about the fact that the United States, from whence began the process of revising these kinds of problems, "had already invented the modern modular kitchen in the nineteenth century. You can see in the movies that a century ago they were already 50 years ahead of Europe."[19] In the early 1930s, however, when the modernizing winds of Rationalism began blowing across Italy, the idea that technology could in some way change not only the manual activities required for the preparation of food but also the very space devoted to those activities still had a futuristic air to it, and was not, therefore, obligatory. Enrico Griffini, author of a famous manual entitled *Costruzione razionale della casa*, published for the first time in 1931 and then reissued many times, seems to betray a certain perplexity at how the Americans were already addressing the issue with great fervor. "In America," he writes, "a true specialization in the rational study of domestic services is being created. The owners of a house in Massachusetts, for example, wishing to rebuild the kitchen, finds it natural to hire a committee of specialists formed by three architects and a lady to devise a solution…. Such a numerous group of skilled individuals would create among us, little accustomed to consider problems of this nature, a certain justified wonderment, and even greater wonderment the result of the solutions, so simple and obvious do they appear. It is a matter of removing certain furniture, moving a sideboard, adding cupboards for pots and pans and shelving for utensils, the demolition of a section of wall, the opening of a door. But all these interventions follow a preordained

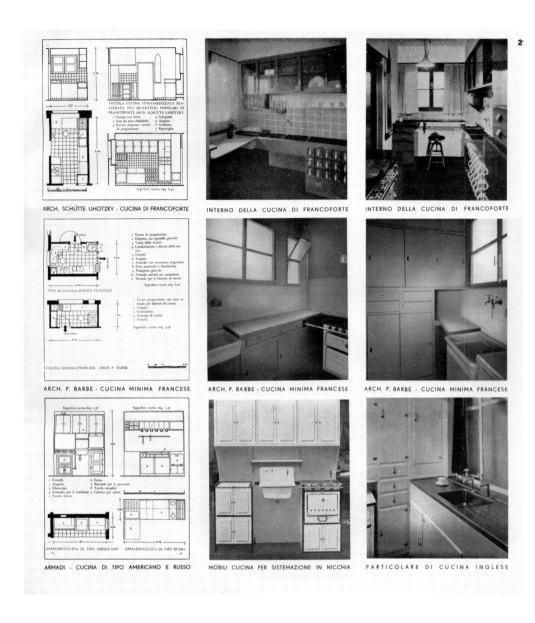

ARCH. SCHÜTTE LIHOTZKY - CUCINA DI FRANCOFORTE | INTERNO DELLA CUCINA DI FRANCOFORTE | INTERNO DELLA CUCINA DI FRANCOFORTE

ARCH. P. BARBE - CUCINA MINIMA FRANCESE | ARCH. P. BARBE - CUCINA MINIMA FRANCESE | ARCH. P. BARBE - CUCINA MINIMA FRANCESE

ARMADI - CUCINA DI TIPO AMERICANO E RUSSO | MOBILI CUCINA PER SISTEMAZIONE IN NICCHIA | PARTICOLARE DI CUCINA INGLESE

plan, with precise directives on the organization of domestic work, with technical diagrams studied carefully to save time and labor."[20] The impression that the Americans, with their lack of a true culinary culture and passion rooted in family life comparable to that of Europe, were changing this and other aspects of household life in a mechanical and indeed 'clinical' way became a widely held opinion, perpetuated in many printed sources. Indeed, Griffini himself found it necessary to point out that these improvements must ensure "in the intention of creating a home where a man can rest, it must also be adapted so that a woman may work."

His rationale for this, hardly revolutionary if read in terms of female emancipation, was that "this is necessary if one wants the modern woman to conserve the tradition of the hearth."[21]

Examining the images collected in 1933 by Giancarlo Palanti in his *Mobili tipici moderni*, one is struck by the traditional aspect of the typologies proposed for the kitchen. There are works by qualified architects—Piero Bottoni, Ettore Sottsass Sr, Gino Pollini, Gio Ponti and others—but they seem to simply stylize with updated lines and forms the older typologies tied to the habits of the hearth, to which Griffini refers. There is

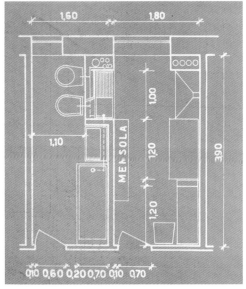

The stasis of the construction industry during the war stimulated redoubled efforts in Italy and Europe to establish precise construction and home-furnishing norms
Top
Subdivision of kitchen work spaces, from M. Zanuso, "Non dimentichiamo la cucina" in *Domus*, May 1944

"Schema di complesso cucina bagno idraulico completo unificato", in *Verso la casa esatta*, Ed It, Milan 1945

an absence of more advanced reflection that would displace the enquiry not so much on the individual furniture item, which is what Palanti documents in his book, with tables, cupboards and sideboards seen as autonomous units to be positioned in ways that make the best use of space, but rather on the principle of the full use of the perimeter surfaces through continuous wall-mounted solutions (such as one finds in the pages of Frenchman Robert Mallet Stevens and German author Martin Elsaesser).[22] Not that everyone in Italy was oblivious to what the architectural avant-garde was doing in this regard. Griffini's book talks extensively about the pioneering kitchen designed by Margarete Schütte-Lihotzky, and at the 4th Monza Triennial in 1930 Piero Bottoni presented a prototype of a kitchen for the "electric house", the most advanced such idea then to be found in Italy, soon to be joined by various other proposals presented at the Milanese Triennials. But the real issue here is that the general technological backwardness of Europe—not just Italy—with regard to electrical appliances impeded the strong and decisive modernization process that would come only after the Second World War, driven by the examples developed by American industry. Everything changed when the refrigerator was acknowledged as having a fundamental role in household administration. But the appliance that would become the object of desire for millions of families did not become widespread in Europe until the 1950s.

The Technological and Typological Evolution of Domestic Life

After the interruption of the Second World War—this was a period of stasis for the construction industry that

however fostered a series of enquiries into standardization ('unification' and 'normalization' were the terms used at the time) that builders and manufacturers would take advantage of in the years to follow—new interest in the kitchen became evident in Italy and the rest of Europe as soon as the war ended, and this was increasingly echoed in print. *Verso la casa esatta*, published in Milan on 30 September 1945, is a collection of essays by various technical experts on the most pressing issues of postwar reconstruction, calling for a shared commitment among designers and manufacturers with regard to "the production of furniture in normalized dimensions," as well as for a revision of the gas and plumbing systems of the bathroom and kitchen. While foreseeing the importance of the kitchen and bath in the domestic landscape of the future, the book provides only the broadest outline, limiting itself to assert that "the kitchen should be a space that is hidden, and which can be therefore maintained in disorder. It should be the most attractive and well-kept part of the home."[23]

An almost exactly contemporary publication, from November 30th, 1945, instead focuses exclusively this topic. *La cucina*, the first volume of a series dedicated to the various areas of the home published by Editoriale Domus, contains a series of reflections which, when read today, establish it as the point of departure of a decades-long process from which Italy would emerge as the key country in every aspect—industrial, cultural and formal—of the kitchen sector.[24] The author is none other than Marco Zanuso, the brilliant architect schooled at the Politecnico di Milano, who was on the verge of becoming one of the great international names in industrial design. Proceeding from a broad historical analysis, Zanuso lists the typical incongruities in the functioning of the traditional kitchen and speaks of "dimensions nearly always large," of "cumbersome heat sources" and the impossibility of "organizing a precise and ordered work area." "Cooking food in a fireplace or with a coal or wood-burning stove," Zanuso adds, "demanded from the housewife not so much precision, but an instinctive ability to improvise and invent. The hygienic problem of cleaning such a space was in the embryonic state; the lack of running water […] necessitated heavy lifting and a significant waste of time. All these negative aspects delayed any scientific approach to the study of this area, and consequently to a better organization of the housewife's duties in the kitchen."

Zanuso did not assume, as had been done in the past, that a woman's work is a value unto itself, but saw it rather as a process to be improved, thus aligning himself with the research being conducted in the context of European Rationalism and American industrial practice. The overall state of things in 1945, however, was still far from any real and widespread progress in the kitchen. "The best products

remain inaccessible to the majority of people, who in the rural areas still continue to employ absolutely primitive methods, while in the cities, though certainly more evolved, the kitchen remains at a level of total inefficiency, technical imprecision, etc. Nearly every kitchen is equipped with furniture produced by hand and without any regard for its function, with dimensions that do not correspond to the objects they are intended to contain. The fixed elements are nothing more than a faucet and drain, and a hearth. Sometimes there is a washbasin and a vent, but these are rare […]. To resolve this problem, it needs to be posed in a radical way. It is necessary to standardize the dimensions of utensils, cookware and furniture so that they might be produced industrially in great numbers […]. Only in this way can all the elements of the kitchen be studied and produced with technical precision and, consequently, with greater efficiency, thereby achieving lower costs that will make them accessible to the masses. In this sense, American industry and technology have already generated significant manufacturing complexes that produce and provide the

Variations on the kitchen layout in the postwar home, from the Swiss journal *Bauen + Wohnen*, February 1948

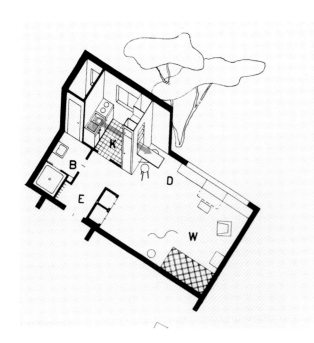

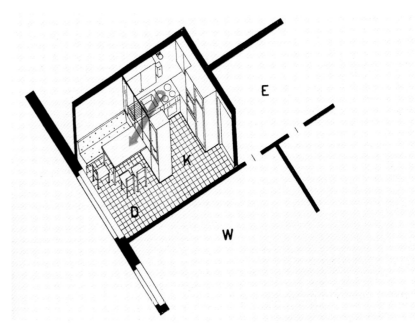

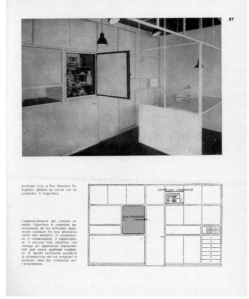

The familiar icon of the
happy housewife, proud
of her household
equipment, is one of the
more ubiquitous images
of the 1950s. Illustration
by Bruno Bellesia, in
*Piccoli segreti della casa
felice*, Officine Grafiche
Mondadori, Verona 1953

market with complete kitchen systems, which, while they have not yet attained absolute precision and efficiency (only because adequate standardization studies have not been done), have nevertheless achieved notably low-cost quantitative and qualitative results that can serve as a model for what will eventually need to be done in Europe."[25] These observations mark the dawn of a dream—the sparkling, metallic dream of the American kitchen, which was to spread across the Western world during the 1950s, even penetrating the societies under Soviet influence.

"As soon as you rise in the morning, unmake the bed or beds, air out the rooms and mattresses. In summer, leave the shutters open a crack, in winter close the windows and open the shutters to let in the sunshine. Prepare and serve breakfast. Rinse the milk bottle and cups and clean the table where breakfast was served. Tidy up the dining room and living room. Throw away the old newspapers, empty the ashtrays, freshen the water in the flower vases, discard any dry flowers. Sweep the floors and then pass over them with a mop, dust the furniture. Close the shutters if necessary.

Straighten up the bedroom, take the clothes you have not worn to the wardrobe or kitchen, brush them down, remove any stains, iron the trousers of your husband and children, replace the clean garments in the closet. Clean the bathroom, wash the toilet, the soap dish and sponge dish, replace the towels if needed, make sure there is enough soap and toothpaste."[26] A lovely itinerary for the housewife's morning, compliments of the 1949 Editoriale Domus yearbook. We move next, naturally, to the kitchen. "Begin preparing the midday meal if the necessary groceries have already been delivered, either by the maid or by the various food vendors. Otherwise, go out and do the shopping. If for some reason you wish to have more of the afternoon free, then by all means prepare something for supper while preparing the midday meal.

After lunch, if you are without a maid, wash the dishes and tidy the kitchen, then set about mending, darning stockings and, the day before ironing day, check the laundry and dampen it. At seven p.m., if you have not had a particularly elaborate lunch, go to the kitchen and prepare as much as necessary and, while supper is cooking,

set the table. Serve the supper and once again, wash the dishes and tidy up the kitchen. Close the gas valves, make sure the entrance door is locked and that the water taps have been left properly closed."[27]

This was the daily reality of millions of housewives, with little variation from region to region, before the advent in the West of the widespread economic expansion often referred to as 'the boom'. Just ten years later, the situation would change profoundly, and the originally insurmountable gap between Europe and the US would in many ways be reduced. The 1959 edition of the same yearbook quoted above reflects this new situation, and is no longer so militaristic in dictating the rhythm of the daily routine.[28] Indeed, it doesn't mention it at all, and goes on instead about entirely different kinds of topics, from 'the crying of children' to the 'history of silverware', from 'beauty for everyone' to 'home fabrics'. And while one advert suggests "for a lively refreshment at home, try sparkling Coca Cola," another from General Electric-owned CGE proudly promotes its wide range of home appliances: "From coffee grinders to more important appliances like refrigerators, not to mention radios and televisions, there

isn't a family today that doesn't use a CGE product."[29]

American Kitchens, European Kitchens

"The 1955 lady of the house is proud of her kitchen, and rightly so, because the kitchen has never been as perfect, shiny and inviting as today [...]. But the American kitchen produced in Italy is slightly modified with respect to the original model. Italian housewives iron their laundry at home, and will not renounce making *tagliatelle* by hand." This statement comes from *La Cucina Italiana*, a glorious magazine founded in 1929 and always quite attentive to the changes in domestic culture that were underway.[30] Not long thereafter, in 1957, the same periodical signaled an interest in kitchens that were "more sober and modest" than the American type, praising a new Danish design then on display at the 9th Triennial in Milan: "It is among those that have enjoyed the greatest success with young people in search of ideas for outfitting a new home [...] [because] the concept of the Danish architects in designing this room was to avoid a clinical style."[31]

By the end of the '50s, a different vision could be glimpsed on the horizon, which

During the '50s, the figure of the housewife altered in parallel with the progressive emancipation of women in Western society, *La Cucina Italiana*, March 1956, July 1954

Opposite
A typically American scene is illustrated here by Ermenegildo Gusmaroli in an advert for CGE appliances, *La Cucina Italiana*, February 1954

The combination of domestic harmony and technological evolution associated collectively with the American kitchen underlies the unrivalled international success it enjoyed throughout the 1950s. This page: illustrations from *House & Garden*, July and October 1949

would then become a true parting of ways between the American and European notions of domestic life—albeit with distinctly different interpretations among the countries of the Old Continent.[32] While the Americans focused on an established and reliable standardization, updated with gadgets and accessories that were always new and apparently indispensable (which helps explain the direct connection between the industrial design of home appliances and the US auto industry, similarly driven by the continuous and conspicuous quest for the new), Europeans began questioning the exaggeration and opulence that had come to be associated with America. Looking back at the Italian print media of the time, one finds numerous indications of this split, which can also be read as a sign of satisfaction for the end of the widespread poverty that followed the war. "Once the economic restrictions of the immediate postwar period and the uncertainties of our own production had been overcome, the lacquered metal American kitchen was held up as an example and imitated on a broad scale. Today, however, it appears to have been left aside and forgotten. Italian taste has asserted itself on the international market with other models, based on other conceptions and structures. Moreover, American production is too distant from our taste, and while its models were copied for many years, today we walk alone, certain as always of our taste and of the validity of our production."[33] In order to respond to the demand for less aggressive lines and layouts than those offered by the Americans—and not bound by the sole principle of

The European response to the kitchens coming out of the United States was essentially imitative until the 1960s, when European designers found new channels of expression
Above
Cucine americane a colori, Görlich, Milan
1958

Right
Detail of a German kitchen, *Schöner Wohnen*, August 1960

At the beginning of the '60s, women's domestic work obligations began to come under discussion, *La Domenica del Corriere*, August 23rd, 1959

perimetral alignment—European designers and manufacturers had to make quite an effort, first copying and assimilating what the US market was constantly churning out, then seeking to formulate their own new combinatory rules and formal proposals. Not long after the end of the war, English adverts were already announcing with a certain optimism that "refrigeration will soon be a common word in every household"[34]—a claim betrayed, however, by the facts, for the presence of home appliances in England, like the rest of Europe, would only approach American levels many years later. In France, as documented in a monographic issue of *L'Architecture d'Aujourd'Hui* from 1947,[35] relatively effective attempts were being made to rationalize the approach to home furnishings and appliances, with significant focus on prefabricated solutions such as '*blocs d'eau*' to be serially inserted into homes. In Germany, which would quickly become a leading country in the field, Poggenpohl went into production

in 1950 with Form 1000, Germany's first industrially produced modular kitchen.[36]

There was movement afoot in Italy as well. The demonstration of "stylistic independence" by Augusto Magnaghi's design of a kitchen for Saffa, "a field in which one often finds imitations of the specific customs of American production," earned a much deserved Golden Compass Award in 1954.[37] Presented that same year was Serie C, designed by Sergio Asti and Sergio Favre for Boffi, a kitchen in lacquered wood with countertops in plastic laminate, handles in cast resin and protective polyester coatings, is remembered as "the beginning of a new Italian discourse on kitchen design."[38] Serie C was important because it embraced the idea of simplicity and orderliness being pursued by a number of designers, often for made-to-measure furniture, as evidenced by various international examples (Ralph Erskine, Maxwell Fry, Raphael S. Soriano, Greta Magnusson Grossmann, Vittorio Borachia, BBPR et.al.) published by

Roberto Aloi in 1952, but which would be assimilated (in part) by industry as a principle of quality only much later.[39] Other noteworthy models from the same company is the T 12 of 1960 by Gian Casè, in which one can recognize a truly Italian touch in the warmth of the wood detailing, and the revolutionary, ultra-compact Minikitchen of 1963 by Joe Colombo. This latter would spark a process of extreme experimentation that continued throughout the '60s and early '70s, including other avant-garde works by Colombo (Visiona 1, 1969; Total Furnishing Unit, 1971), Experiment 70 by Luigi Colani (prototype realized by Poggenpohl and presented at the Cologne Furniture Fair of 1970)[40] and other designs where practicality was combined with the futuristic/psychedelic attitudes then in fashion.[41]

Even earlier, from the very beginning of the 1960s, there was work being done on minimal, compact volumes fractioned into modular units or combined in a single block, resulting in products of excellent formal quality. One such example is the Serie 2000 by Poggenpohl, presented in Cologne in 1962, which introduced a profound innovation by substituting handles with a continuous groove for opening the doors and drawers.[42] This approach was particularly successful in Italy, starting with the Unibloc kitchen by Makio Hasuike for Ariston Merloni (1962–68), continuing then with Marco Zanuso's E5 for Elam (1966), the S60 series by Claudio Salocchi for Alberti (1967), Timo by Vico Magistretti for Schiffini (1971), Luigi Massoni's designs for Boffi, and eventually arriving at the present day.

Much like the automobile industry, the modular kitchen sector gradually came to be organized as a creative and entrepreneurial process, where the mechanism that leads to the invention of new models and subsequent standardization is generated almost as if by osmosis between design and business.

One Day in the Early '60s, in Pesaro...

It is against this background of experimentation and enquiry that the Scavolini adventure began. Founded by the determination and perseverance of young Valter—nineteen years old when he decided to start his own business after having acquired manufacturing experience in a small local factory—and later joined by his brother Elvino, the company began operating according to the guidelines followed by other Italian and European manufacturers. Starting in the mid-'40s, and above all from the following decade onward, Pesaro and environs established itself as a catalyst in the geography of 'industrial districts' that accompanied the growth and maturation of the Italian industrial system. The area's specialty was furniture, which placed it in competition with other areas with a similar vocation in Lombardy, Tuscany, the Veneto and Friuli-Venezia Giulia. The Scavolini brothers, with a difference in age of eleven years but with shared experience in manufacturing, spent their childhood in a context that witnessed the transition from artisanal production to full-fledged industrial manufacturing. It was natural, therefore, that the two young men, alert and motivated, should attempt such a big entrepreneurial leap in those years which, like all pioneering epochs everywhere, are exciting precisely because they are so full of unknowns and, consequently, possibilities. It was in this period that Italy, at least in part, had begun to shed its heritage of centuries of poverty, embarking on the path toward a widespread, if controversial, modernization.

More than anything else, the Scavolini brothers worked very hard. All day, every day, including Saturdays and Sundays. And all the while they

watched and learned. "We began
producing composite furniture for the
kitchen, like sideboards, or as we used
to call them, buffets," recalls Valter
Scavolini. "But then, as has been the
case ever since, we didn't just stay
where we were. We looked around, we
saw what worked on the market. We
recognized the growing interest in a
new type of kitchen based on modules,
coordinated by decoration and
dimensions, to be combined and
repeated according to one's needs, and
we said alright, let's give it a try."[43] Like
many other Italian companies in the
field that sprang up and evolved during
those years from their original artisanal

configuration, the group that Scavolini
targeted was the typical family,
attracted by products that were modern,
yes, but not too aggressive, tempered by
references to tradition. Indeed, since the
mid-1960s the 'rustic' kitchen—
equipped with the latest appliances but
styled in wood or fake wood with
moldings and beaded trim—has
occupied a stable market niche.[44]
The first modular kitchen manufactured
by Scavolini was called Svedese (1962),
which was immediately followed by
Finest.[45] Faced in plastic laminate, they
are carefully constructed and minutely
detailed, such as the narrow contrasting
strip/handle of Finest and, in this same

Interiors and exteriors of the Scavolini plant in Montelabbate, a few miles from Pesaro

Above, three images of the production area as it was in the '70s; below, the farmland later used for the plant's expansion, pictured here in 1976

This page
Three photos of the plant taken in 1985 and new offices, 1996

Some of the earliest
models produced by
Scavolini. From upper left,
clockwise: Finest (Studio
Vuesse, 1963), Italia
(Studio Vuesse, 1963),
Color Studio Vuesse,
1969), Flower (Studio
Vuesse, 1967)

Right and bottom
The austerity of the L'Isola
della Melarosa model
(Agostino Bertani, 1975)

model, the rounded edges made possible by then new techniques for machining laminate, of which the company immediately availed itself. The tapered metal feet that raise the modules off the floor, elongated to become table legs, are part of the stylistic heritage of the '50s that was still in use in the new decade. Not long thereafter came the Italia kitchen,[46] similar to the previous two in overall design, which could be defined as Scandinavian with the softening influence of Italian taste. In a later version from 1967, the metal feet were replaced by elements in lathe-turned wood that made its encounter with the floor more harmonious.

With Flower (1967), color made a more decisive appearance, with versions in sand and chrome yellow that contrasted with details and hardware in walnut-tinted laminate to create a sober and elegant model, clearly Italian in tone. The 1960s closed with Color, a kitchen that revisits forms and stylistic motifs of the past and that marks the launch of a long and successful line of similar models, from Connye (1975, one of the

all-time bestsellers), Fanny (1982), Dolly (1983), Melissa (1990) and numerous others. Constructed like Flower in hollow-core with laminate facing, Color owes its retro look to the wavy profile of the frames that surround the mirrored doors and drawers.

Sustained by the steady faith of its clientele, during the mid-'70s Scavolini introduced an important change of course with respect to what it had been doing thus far. After a decade and a half of fully in-house design, the company management decided that the time had come to entrust outside designers with some of its products. In 1975, Agostino Bertani, the first, proposed the aforementioned Connye and L'Isola della Melarosa, a kitchen of exceptional formal grace that eliminated drawer and door handles in favor of recesses carved into the top edges and that came in a range of captivating colors like daffodil white, clivia red and monsoon grey. After Bertani, who went on to produce other designs for the company, Dante Benini

Merry (Dante Benini,
1978)

Opposite
Lucciola (Agostino
Bertani, 1980), carrying
the first official Scavolini
logo

was enlisted in 1978 to create the
Happy and Merry models, the first a
warm and rustic composition in natural
pine, the second clean and simple. That
same year, Simone Donato designed
L'Elite. 1982 was the year of Enrico
Tonucci's Trapezio, a fresh and
contemporary alternative to existing
schemes addressed to a young, non-
conformist clientele. Along with them
came other designers, called upon by
Scavolini to update the classic-
traditional line (Simone Donato,
Roberto Ciolli) and the more modern
one (Pierluigi Molinari, Silvano
Barsacchi), although without deviating
too conspicuously from a certain

established image that the company had
no intention of renouncing, and which
the in-house design office, Studio
Vuesse, continued to maintain. The
collaboration in the early '90s with
Jonathan De Pas, Donato D'Urbino and
Paolo Lomazzi, creators of Gemma
(1991), a kitchen featuring curved,
modulating profiles, and Roberto Lucci
and Paolo Orlandini, who designed
Mimsy (1991), along with regular
collaborators Gianni Pareschi, Giuliano
Cappelletti and Enzo Pozzoli, was the
prelude to a change in direction toward
a more contemporary approach, which
would be the main strategy of the
following decade.[47]

lucciola
DESIGN: A. BERTANI

SCAVOLINI
CUCINE S.P.A.

93

Gennaio

Sugli automezzi per le strade italiane, corre veloce il marchio Scavolini.

SCAVOLINI

la cucina più amata dagli italiani

With the growth of revenues and consolidation on the national market, images of Scavolini trucks carrying kitchens across Italy became popular, as in this promotional postcard from 1987–88

Scavolini and the History of Italian Advertising

She enters the scene like the queen of the home. She faces the camera and winks, a cross between a high-class housewife and a star. Her glamorous clothing and elaborate hairstyle, though clearly belonging to a long-ago fashion, remain impressed on the memory at first sight. A memorable chapter in the history of Italian advertising and custom was opened between 1984 and 1986 when Raffaella Carrà, the most famous showgirl in the country at the time, shot a series of television ads for Scavolini providing testimonials for the company. It was a moment when the brand from Pesaro had reached its highest revenues ever, and was now solidly the foremost kitchen manufacturer in Italy. "I had read in a popular magazine that Raffaella, along with President of the Republic Sandro Pertini and Pope John Paul II, was the most beloved public figure in Italy," recalls Valter Scavolini. "So we decided to contact her and asked her to work for us."[48] During those years, Raffaella Carrà was the epitome of what was called 'general' television. It was a stroke of genius on the part of the Scavolini brothers, a demonstration of marketing talent and business acumen. The impact of the famous slogan "*la più amata dagli italiani*" (which translates roughly to 'The best seller from Italy', referring to both the implicit feminine noun '*cucina*' and to Ms. Carrà herself) is so encompassing as to be still well-remembered today. The tie between advertising and kitchen manufacture has distant origins. Since the dawn of industrial production, companies have tried to promote their products by targeting their communications at homemakers and nuclear families, often deploying the 'dream' associated with such imagery. This started in the print media and then made its way to

television. In Italy, the earliest (and rare) TV ads for kitchens and appliances were seen toward the end of the 1950s on "Carosello," the famous variety show, which was saturated with advertising. Zanussi and Zoppas proposed their products steadily throughout the '60s and '70s, and Salvarani broadcast a conspicuous series of promotional episodes between 1968 and 1976.[49] Scavolini joined the television bandwagon in 1975 with spots featuring the animated figure of *Il Cuochino,* or 'Little Chef'. During the '80s, with the arrival of new private television networks alongside the state-run RAI, television presence became a marketing necessity, particularly for reaching the audience that did not habitually read newspapers and magazines. It was at this time that the concept of a 'famous person' assumed a more direct role in communications with the public. It was no longer a question of trumpeting the virtues of a product with a circumlocutory narration, which had been the norm for "Carosello," but to urge the viewer and potential customer into recognizing themselves, with the help of the right company representative, in the circumstances of everyday life depicted in the advert. What was new, however, in the way that Scavolini proposed its kitchens through Raffaella Carrà was both the size of the investment—for we are not talking about the occasional ad, but a massive, targeted campaign that immediately drew a huge audience—and the cultural significance of the operation. When all is said and done, the idea of transforming a television celebrity into a housewife (the message is, in truth, somewhat ambiguous, insofar as Raffaella Carrà was not presented as a woman accustomed to housework, and her look is meticulously styled,[50] but perhaps that is precisely why it works) was one of the most effective *mises-en-scène* in the dramatization of kitchen life since the distant 1950s. Transformed into an

The character of *Il Cuochino* marked Scavolini's debut in the Italian television advertising system in 1975

Opposite
Raffaella Carrà, queen of Italian television and star of a series of famous spots for Scavolini from 1984 to 1986.
Ad campaign featuring the Fairy kitchen (Studio Vuesse, 1986)

The transformation of the
television diva into a
sophisticated homemaker
was interpreted perfectly
by Raffaella Carrà, and
cast the myth of the
happy 1950s housewife
in a postmodern light.
Ad campaign from 1984
featuring Fiordaliso
(Studio Vuesse, 1983)

101

Promotional postcards
signaling the transition
of Scavolini's advertising
to television with Raffaella
Carrà, 1984

ethereal energy field by the cathode tube, Raffaella Carrà was the dream version of the proud and happy postwar housewife. "And here is Raffaella, in a splendid setting along with a Scavolini kitchen, who presents herself once again to the audience, complicitous in a new dress. Walking the entire length of the dazzling kitchen, she turns to the audience with bright spontaneity: 'Success and applause are always such a pleasure…which is why they must be deserved…like Scavolini, who make kitchens the way we Italians like them: beautiful, carefully detailed, fully equipped, with solutions suited to every family and fine materials, chosen to last.'"[51] A perfect transcription of that atmosphere is the model from 1984 named for Ms. Carrà: Raffaella, lacquered to a pearlescent patina, apparently

embodying upper-class decor but in reality affordable by many—such is that world and that culture from which it takes inspiration.

Between the '80s and '90s, Scavolini's image was given a further boost by a fresh and sophisticated new graphic approach developed by Massimo Dolcini for the entire range of company publications, such as the journals of the Fondazione Scavolini (instituted in 1984), the pamphlets on the various kitchen models and other publishing initiatives, like the lovely monograph of 1992 that commemorated the company's first 30 years. But television would remain the driving force of Scavolini's communications strategy. When Raffaella Carrà's reign as Scavolini representative ended in 1987, a fresh new face arrived to

la cucina più amata dagli italiani

SCAVOLINI

Tutti amano lo stile italiano, il nostro modo di vivere
di saperci circondare di cose belle.
Una cucina Scavolini è italiana nel gusto
nella fantasia, nella praticità delle soluzioni.
È per questo che tutti la amiamo.

Raffaella Carrà fa scoprire
la qualità e i dettagli
delle cucine Scavolini.

Nel filmato Raffaella, rivolta
confidenzialmente al pubblico attraverso
la macchina da presa, illustra ora la
qualità e i pregi delle cucine Scavolini.

Trapezio (Enrico Tonucci, 1982), one of the most innovative models in Scavolini's back catalogue

convey the company's philosophy: Lorella Cuccarini, an emerging star in the world of Italian television, respected and appreciated for her natural simplicity and modesty.[52] She was the ideal person to provide testimonials for Scavolini. Her reputation as a wholesome and dynamic young woman, with a look and manner inspired at first by the pop iconography of *Flashdance*, made it possible to translate the image of 'family brand', very important to the company during this period, in a contemporary key. She was so perfect for the role that she played it uninterruptedly until 2004.

With a remarkable ability to read its audience, Scavolini continued throughout this long period to detect and interpret the ever-changing signals of social and cultural transformation. Indeed, the way in which Lorella Cuccarini's role and look changed over the years is a faithful

record of the company's efforts to stay in tune with its clientele. Following the original youthful/athletic Cuccarini, came the first 'revision': "dazzling, confident, seductive,"[53] a Cuccarini that had grown up and blossomed into a woman. The settings of the adverts were no longer dance backgrounds, but proper kitchens. A fairytale component infiltrated the narratives of the ads: "In the white Alison kitchen [a model designed by Silvano Barsacchi from 1989], Lorella's guests are delightful little ducks that march out adorably in line, then end up investigating every corner of the kitchen...who can resist such cuteness?"[54] In 1992 Lorella Cuccarini began appearing in print adverts in a three-quarter pose next to the kitchen being promoted, her smiling face in soft focus. By mid-decade, there was another revision toward a greater overall

Lorella (Silvano
Barsacchi, 1988), a
kitchen that took its name
from the new Scavolini
testimonial

Below
Advertising campaign
1989, the Lucilla kitchen
(Studio Vuesse, 1989)

sobriety. Cuccarini was then presented
frontally wearing an elegant red tube
dress, sexy but tasteful, her blonde hair
framing her face. This was more or less
the look that she would maintain until
2004, the only significant change being
the color of the dress, which went from
red to black in 2002–03. The original and
very successful slogan, "*la più amata
dagli italiani*", accompanied the entire
communication campaign like a mantra,

either on its own or combined with
various payoffs: "*più vicina alla gente,
più amata dagli italiani*" (1998—which
roughly means 'the closest to people,
the best seller from Italy'), "*una Scavolini
è autentica...come te*" (2001–02—'a
Scavolini kitchen is authentic...like you'),
"*io tengo per le cose vere, autentiche...io
tengo per Scavolini*" (2002–04—'I prefer
things that are real, authentic...I prefer
Scavolini').

Lorella Cuccarini and the Raffaella kitchen (Studio Vuesse, 1984), during the shooting of a spot for the 1987 advertising campaign

Lietta (Silvano Barsacchi,
1990), a kitchen that
incorporates a wide range
of possibilities for
customization

Above
The soft volumes of
Gemma (Jonathan De
Pas, Donato D'Urbino,
Paolo Lomazzi, 1991)

Left
Dandy (Studio Vuesse,
1985), the biggest seller
in the company's history

Starting in the late 1960s, several Scavolini models interpreted the widespread nostalgia that was beginning to infiltrate the modular kitchen market. Pictured here is Beatrice (Roberto Ciolli, 1991)

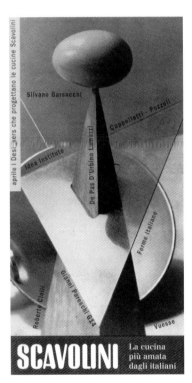

Promotional postcards,
1993

From Italian Trademark to Global Brand

The current structure of the Scavolini company, discussed at the beginning of this book, began to be defined in the second half of the 1990s. The heritage of the first thirty years is reflected in this new phase at various levels, insofar as the stimuli for facing the challenges of a rapidly evolving market in a proactive way came from the experience and professionalism that had been acquired in the past. After the success of the 1980s, Scavolini had become a solid economic success story with a strong business vision, accustomed to operate with a diversified and targeted strategy in terms of product, industrial innovation and communication. The decision to go with spokeswomen had proven to be a smart one, and for this reason continued well to the 2004. However, there were many changes afoot, and at a certain point the need for a significant change in direction became clear: Scavolini had to renew the perceived image of the brand and provide new products that responded to the changing expectations of its customers.

After the ephemeral ostentation of the '80s, the kitchen manufacturing industry underwent a profound transformation. There was a general desire for order and formal economy, for a return to the original principles of design, and this was tied to an increased interest in culinary technique and culture. The ease of travel combined with the growing migratory flow towards the West broadened people's curiosity about the flavors of the world. And along with the fascination with the exotic came the rediscovery of the incredible wealth of local gastronomic tradition, from which Italy's 'slow food' revolution was born. All of this had significant repercussions for the kitchen industry. The model that everyone wanted, sometimes to the point of exaggeration, was the high-performance hotel kitchen. The decorative exhibitionism of the '80s was replaced in the following decade by the aesthetic of industrial minimalism. Technology was in part to blame, for it began providing homes with high-quality professional tools that pandered to people's culinary exploits.

During these years, Scavolini produced a series of models that interpreted the widespread attraction for the laboratory-style kitchen. A return to the desire for natural materials and colors combined with the growing minimalist ethos that served as a counterpoint to the persistence of traditional stylistic memes, quite apparent in the Beatrice model of 1991 by Roberto Ciolli. Three kitchens from the early '90s—Malva (Ciolli), Petunia (Giuliano Cappelletti and Enzo Pozzoli) and Ambra (Silvano Barsacchi)—play on these combinations to endow the models with a sense of security and reliability. This dualism continued throughout the decade, with reassuringly 'familiar' models like Mirto and Silene (Roberto Ciolli, 1992, 1993), Domobel and Darling (Raffaello Pravato, 1995, 1998),[55] and the slimmer builds of Verbena (Gianni Pareschi, 1992), Gilia (Cappelletti and Pozzoli, 1993), Oxalis (Silvano Barsacchi, 1993), Ninfea (Studio Vuesse, 1994) and Farm (again Gianni Pareschi, 1995). A clear synthesis of this line of enquiry is Baltimora, a model designed by Studio Vuesse in collaboration with Marco Pareschi (1998), for the balanced way the memory of the past is translated into the forms and taste of the present. With Tess, designed by Silvano Barsacchi in 1998, we instead enter directly into the spartan aesthetic of the new millennium, for it embodies the concept of the sculptural, geometric kitchen and prefigures the Scavolini models of the latest generation.

Starting in 1996, with the launch of the new brand Ernestomeda, controlled by

A progressive tendency toward simplification that did not, however, preclude the warmth of the past was a recurring ethos in Scavolini's kitchens of the 1990s, like Petunia (Giuliano Cappelletti, Enzo Pozzoli, 1992)

Scavolini but entirely autonomous in terms of management and production and positioned differently on the market, the need for an overall jump in quality became clear. The success of Ernestomeda, which came rapidly and abundantly in terms of revenues, is based on the parameters that are the lifeblood of Scavolini: professionalism, high-quality products and competitive prices.

The ingredients were the same, but the difference was that, by comparison with the formal experimentalism and contemporary design of Ernestomeda, Scavolini's predominant goal is to satisfy the demand of a much larger client base with more eclectic tastes.

The administration of this phase was entrusted to a new generation of management: the children of Valter and Elvino Scavolini—Alberto, Emanuela, Fabiana and Gian Marco—and Vittorio Renzi, who had guided Ernestomeda to

success before moving on in 2003 to become the CEO of the parent company. Market research enabled the new team to determine precisely the margins of maneuver for a new long-term strategy for Scavolini, which can be summed up in a decisive move toward the technological and aesthetic prospects of the future, to be conducted, however, without any radical breaks or sudden changes that would disorient the more traditional clientele.[56] This new path was developed by pursuing several areas of research. The sociological approach is based on the attentive analysis of the aesthetic and practical expectations of specific socio-cultural groups. The experimental approach is aimed instead at identifying new ideas through open research on the relationships between the kitchen and the everyday rituals of the people who spend time in them.[57] Lastly, there is the area of pure design research, whose

An image from the
Scavolini company ad,
2005

purpose is to continually update the
diversified Scavolini product catalogue.
All of this has reflected directly on the
choices made in recent years to confer a
more recognizable dimension to the
brand. The retirement of Lorella
Cuccarini in 2004 and a rethinking of the
company's entire communication
strategy[58] led to the launch in 2005 of a
new campaign that placed the Scavolini
brand and product at the centre of the
message for the first time. Debuting in
the spring of that year and running for a
long while on the main Italian networks,
with the usual support from print, radio
and movie theatre ads, the campaign
deployed sophisticated contemporary
narrative memes, far from the
stereotypical adverts for the home. The
star was now the kitchen itself, the only
perfectly furnished space in a context

that the viewer glimpsed as a household:
a large, inviting kitchen with adjoining
dining area—the model in this case is the
new Glam, designed by Marco Pareschi,
in dark wood and aluminum—which was
presented as the ideal backdrop for the
everyday rituals of a young family. The
message, accompanied by the sounds of
Bert Kaempfert's *L-O-V-E*, is simple and
clear: this is the beating heart of the
home, the space to best enjoy the simple
but intense pleasures of daily life.[59]
"Whatever your home is like… if you
have a Scavolini there's more taste in the
kitchen" is the message that closes the
spot. In 2009 a new campaign is
developed—seven stories for different
audiences. In the wake of the slogan
"You can always expect the best from a
Scavolini kitchen" and against a
soundtrack of Irving Berlin's timeless

Scavolini Store Milano, in
Viale Enrico Martini, which
opened in December
2009

Below
The Scavolini sales point
that opened in Shanghai
in October 2010

Cheek to Cheek, it was presented as a live webcast to the media and own dealers. The intention was to create a circuit that would both communicate and foster cultural growth, so that the Scavolini customer is offered not just a kitchen but a set of ethical values in keeping with the brand's history. The new promotional strategy is interwoven with deep interventions on the level of distribution and new product design.

The process of selecting and preparing the points of sale is proceeding through a reinforcement of the entire network of dealers in Italy and abroad. The latest step is the opening of the mono-brand Scavolini Stores in support (not in substitution) of the existing sales network. From the production standpoint, in 2003 the key points of the preceding years came together in the launch of the "cheap and chic" line, Scavolini Basic, as well as in the decision to increasingly involve internationally renowned designers alongside the company's long-time collaborators. The first was Giugiaro Design, who came up with Flux (2007), a kitchen with a strong technological impact that nonetheless presents itself to the user with a friendly, non-aggressive image. Soon thereafter came Perry King and Santiago Miranda, who devised a solution to the unresolved problem of the

'conceptual' positioning of the kitchen within the home. Their idea was to emphasize the scenographic power that a good kitchen can exert, making it the fulcrum of the entire domestic hierarchy. The ethnic flavor of Marcello Cutino's designs is another recent and stimulating direction of enquiry, as are the 'cool' graphics of Karim Rashid and the modular ideas of Michael Young, which we mentioned earlier in the book.

New market realities, along with Scavolini's strong expansion into foreign markets, have necessitated a major transformation of the company in both organizational and technological terms. The decision to focus on products that are ever more customizable, from dimensions to function to aesthetics (indeed, all production is now done exclusively to order), requires maintaining firm control over each order, which must pass through the entire supply chain (dealers, company, suppliers) as rapidly as possible. This has in turn necessitated the installation of equipment and organizational procedures that are practically futuristic in comparison with the rest of the sector, such as the amazing robotized vertical storage facilities.[60]

And the rest, at the moment of writing, is history that has yet to be made.

Il successo bisogna meritarselo... Come Scavolini che fa le cucine come le amiamo noi italiani: belle, curate nei particolari, complete di tutto, con soluzioni adatte ad ogni famiglia e con materiali scelti per durare.

SCAVOLINI
la più amata dagli italiani

Left and below
The evolution of the Scavolini advertising message from the era of celebrity representatives to today

Una Scavolini è autentica ...come te

Baltimora (Studio Vuesse with Marco Pareschi, 1999), with its subtle reinterpretation of traditional iconography, is still one of Scavolini's flagship models today

Pages 124–5
The minimalist sensibility of Tess (Silvano Barsacchi, 1999 prefigured the climate of the new millennium

Economy of form and
practicality of use are the
key features of Glam
(Marco Pareschi, 2005)

[1] Valter Scavolini, 2010. Statement recorded at the Scavolini plant in Montelabbate (Pesaro), March 2010.

[2] *Company Policy of the Scavolini Group*, first edition February 1996, viewable on the company website.

[3] Scavolini's collaboration with Italian designers began in 1974. Currently, the designers working with the company (along with those cited above) are Silvano Barsacchi, Marcello Cutino, Gianni Pareschi, Marco Pareschi and Raffaello Pravato.

[4] The name is a tribute to the famous video game, Tetris.

[5] Eurocucina is the biennial trade show for kitchens, held since 1974 at the same time as the Milan Furniture Fair (founded in 1961). Scavolini was present at the first show, and then every year since 1978.

[6] This is also the approach of the new Atelier model (Studio Vuesse), 2010.

[7] Video viewable on the Scavolini website.

[8] Valter Scavolini, 2010.

[9] Viewable on the Scavolini website. It is significant that these observations come from Gianni Pareschi, creator of iconic works of contemporary design (the *Baffo* chair, with Ezio Didone, 1969; *Libro*, with Umberto Orsoni, 1970; *Fiocco*, 1970). The Absolute Classic collection is composed of the *Baccarat*, *Grand Relais* and *Long Island* models.

[10] Valter Scavolini, 2010.

[11] From the in-house document *Scavolini and its Dealers*, 2010.

[12] Scavolini designs the showrooms and provides dealers with dedicated software (updatable online) for graphic design and order development that interfaces with the internal SAP system. This optimizes the company processes, integrates communications between the various participating commercial partners, and assists the dealer when formulating orders with qualified personnel (agents). Training focuses on giving dealers up-to-date knowledge of all the options and possibilities of Scavolini products. In 1994 the first 'Growing Together' workshops were instituted; since 2010 the company web portal has offered the 'Scavolini Academy' e-learning service.

[13] The current Scavolini network includes more than 150 points of sale in Europe, more than 60 in Russia and the neighboring republics, 30 in North America, 25 in Central and South America, and 20 in Asia and Oceania. The rapidly developing African continent already has 6 showrooms, and others are slated to open soon.

[14] From the in-house document *Scavolini Stores*, April 2010. "Scavolini Stores are run by independent distributors who wish to seize commercial opportunities by relying on the image and distinction that the Scavolini organization can offer."

[15] Alberto Capatti, Massimo Montanari, *La cucina italiana. Storia di una cultura*, Laterza, Rome–Bari 1999.

[16] Pellegrino Artusi, *La scienza in cucina e l'arte di mangiare bene*. Landi, Florence 1891.

[17] Catharine E. Beecher, Harriet Beecher Stowe, *American Woman's Home*, J.B. Ford & Co., New York 1869.

[18] Agostino Feria, *Saggio di nomenclatura domestica italiana parlata e definita*, Paravia, Florence-Milan-Turin 1870.

[19] Valter Scavolini, 2010.

[20] Enrico A. Griffini, *Costruzione razionale della casa*, 2nd ed., Hoepli, Milan 1933.

[21] *Ibid.*

[22] *Mobili tipici moderni*, Giancarlo Palanti ed., Editoriale Domus, Milan 1933.

[23] The views of Gio Ponti (one of the authors) can be recognized here; *Verso la casa esatta*, Guido Beretta, Pietro Giulio Bosisio, Adalberto Libera, Gio Ponti, Pierangelo Pozzi, Eugenio Soncini, Giuseppe Vaccaro, Carlo Villa, Ed It, Milan 1945.

[24] Marco Zanuso, *La cucina*, Editoriale Domus, Milan 1945.

[25] *Ibid.*

[26] *Libro di casa 1949*, Editoriale Domus, Milan 1948.

[27] *Ibid.*

[28] *Libro di casa 1959*, Editoriale Domus, Milan 1958.

[29] *Ibid.*

[30] "La cucina di oggi", *La Cucina Italiana*, April 1955.

[31] "I mobili presentati alla Triennale", *La Cucina Italiana*, October 1957. Not that the Americans failed to consider this change of course with respect to the excessive, metallic uniformity of the previous phase, as the following passage from the December 1959 issue of *House & Garden* demonstrates: "The kitchens most of us love and remember best are those which appeal to all our senses. Memory calls up the spicy smell of drying herbs, the comforting crackle of the fire, the friendly textures of wood and brick. Naturally we would never forego the carefree qualities of modern equipment, but we do hanker after the best of both worlds."

[32] Also contributing to this is the level reached by the European home appliance industry, which from the early 1960s became capable of operating independently of transatlantic technology.

[33] *Casa Nuova*, "Guida pratica all'arredamento", issue 7, "La cucina", March 2nd, 1967. Similar reflections are found in a slightly later text, *I mille consigli di casa mia* (Mario Oriani, Gruppo Editoriale Corriere della Sera, Milan 1969): "After the war, in the wake of the American market, we began building fitted kitchens in Italy, too, clean and white, with surfaces of colored Formica and chrome-legged chairs and tables. Then, gradually, our architects and designers took an interest in the problem and began to create a more European, more Italian kitchen; softer, gentler, with wood alongside the plastic and a less rigid structure."

[34] *The Architectural Review*, August 1946 (Prestcold Refrigeration). "Regular and adequate deliveries of built-in refrigerators will be available from January 1947 for housing schemes": this is the promise of an Electrolux advert from the October issue of the same magazine. New solutions for the home and kitchen, along with consumer goods for the English society of the future, were presented in London in the autumn of 1946 by the exhibition "Britain Can Make It", held at the Victoria & Albert Museum.

[35] *L'Architecture d'Aujourd'Hui*, monographic issue, "L'equipement de l'habitation", March 1947. It is interesting to note how, in listing the most advanced solutions for industrially produced kitchens available at the time, only the English, Swedish, American and French are mentioned. Notably absent are the Ger-

mans, due to obvious postwar obstacles, and the Italians, who were slower to embrace change.

[36] *100 Jahre Poggenpohl. Tradition, die in die Zukunft wirkt*, PPK, Bielefeld 1992.

[37] First presentation of the Golden Compass Award, 1954. The jury was composed of Aldo Borletti, Cesare Brustio, Gio Ponti, Alberto Rosselli and Marco Zanuso.

[38] *In cucina. Con un vero arredamento*, Giancarlo Iliprandi (ed.), Görlich, Milan 1974.

[39] Roberto Aloi, *L'arredamento moderno*, Hoepli, Milan 1952. An example of this simplicity, still indebted to American iconography, is the kitchen designed in 1957 in England by George Fejér for Hygena; *Designers in Britain 5*, André Deutsch Ltd, London 1957; June Freeman, *The Making of the Modern Kitchen. A Cultural History*, Berg, Oxford-New York 2004.

[40] *100 Jahre Poggenpohl*, 1992.

[41] An example is the Renoform VX 600 by Alno (1973); *Möbeldesign. Mobili tedeschi dal 900 a oggi*, Design Center Stuttgart (ed.), Maisch & Queck, Gerlingen 1985.

[42] *100 Jahre Poggenpohl*. Another German model distinguished for the cleanliness of its lines, designed by Norbert Schlagheck and Odo Klose for Husser in 1961; *Möbeldesign. Mobili tedeschi dal 900 a oggi*.

[43] Valter Scavolini, 2010. Regarding the typology of the modular kitchen, this is the definition provided by a text from 1967: "The criterion of modularity, which has influenced in such a significant way the look of the modern kitchen, arose from the need to confer a homogeneous character to this space which does away with any contrast between the appliances and the furniture. The idea was to 'align' the various elements and 'compose' them so that they created the most harmonious possible whole." *Abitare oggi*, Pietro Toschi and Franco Magnani (eds.), Görlich, Milan 1967.

[44] "Wood, which had been all but banned (in the earliest modular kitchens, ed.) gradually began to reappear, softening the lines of the furniture. The new materials—metals, synthetic resins, plastic facings, etc.—lost their early coldness and tried to adapt to this new demand. It is a return to tradition, but one that exploits all the possibilities placed at our disposal by technological progress and by the production of various elements on an industrial scale." *Abitare oggi* 1967.

[45] Unless otherwise indicated, the dates given in the text refer to the year a given model went into production. The register at the end of the book indicates both the year the model was designed and the year it went into production.

[46] Valter Scavolini has always been involved in the design process, at first directly and later in constant collaboration with the design team. Carlo Viglino, head of the in-house design studio and with Scavolini since 1980, says, "It's a job I've always done and continue to do with his help. Valter Scavolini 'feels' the products like they're his own children; he knows every technical and industrial aspect perfectly. He's certainly not the type to stay behind a desk. He's a man of action who loves to contribute to the creation of new models." (Carlo Viglino, spoken testimony, July 2010).

[47] This process can also be seen in the progressive simplification of one of Scavolini's most prolific designers, Silvano Barsacchi (Lorella, 1987, Tess, 1998, Vega, 1999, Mood, 2005).

[48] Valter Scavolini, 2010.

[49] Marco Giusti, *Il grande libro di Carosello*, Sperling & Kupfer, Milan 1995.

[50] Attention to this aspect is emphasized in a passage describing the 1986 campaign: "In the film, Scavolini tends to the tiniest detail of the image. And Raffaella now presents herself to the audience with perfect and extremely elegant clothes by the top designers, a new coiffure and sophisticated makeup", *La nuova campagna pubblicitaria Scavolini e Raffaella Carrà simboli di successo di uno stile tutto italiano*, corporate publication, 1986.

[51] Excerpt from the first spot featuring Raffaella Carrà for Scavolini in 1984; *La cucina più amata dagli italiani*, corporate publication, 1984.

[52] A model of kitchen was named after her as well. Designed by Silvano Barsacchi, the kitchen is characterised by clean, simple lines and an honest practicality.

[53] *La nuova campagna pubblicitaria della Scavolini. La cucina come emozione*, corporate publication, 1989.

[54] *Ibid.*

[55] The new Absolute Classic collection by Gianni Pareschi revisits this line.

[56] "We cannot allow ourselves to try and please only certain inclinations of taste. We must remember that alongside those who love the modern and the contemporary are those who cannot do without the reassurance of classic traditional design. This compels us to avoid taking steps that are too reckless, for otherwise we'll scare off a whole swath of our clientele and lose their loyalty. This has happened before, and we've learned the lesson. But neither can we allow ourselves to lag behind, because our numbers must always be at the top. It's not easy, clearly, but I think that we all know how to do our jobs well." Carlo Viglino, 2010.

[57] In this regard, between 2005 and 2006, in collaboration with ADI (Association for Industrial Design), the first Scavolini Kitchens Workshop was organized, involving around 20 young Italian designers who presented their results in June 2006 at the Milan Triennial exhibition.

[58] In 1997, after the launch of Ernestomeda, the Komma agency of Milan began to manage the Scavolini advertising.

[59] The setting prefigures the expansion of the kitchen to the living area that Scavolini would develop shortly thereafter with Scenery by Perry King and Santiago Miranda.

[60] From this, the Assist project was created with the aim of integrating all processes in an efficient way through the use of advanced computer technology and perfectly calibrated organizational strategy.

Massimo Martignoni,
Valentina Dalla Costa

Scavolini:
A Chronology 1931–2011

Unless otherwise indicated, citations are taken from Scavolini catalogues or the company website. The accounts relating to the company's history and the Scavolini family were collected over the course of 2010

Elvino Scavolini, 1958

Valter Scavolini, 1959

1931

November 1st: Elvino Scavolini is born in Pesaro to a family of sharecroppers, Guerrino (1904–1996) and Teresa née Scatassa (1911–1982). From 1962 on, Elvino would work alongside his younger brother, Valter.

1942

January 8th: Valter Scavolini is born in Pesaro.

1950–1955

Elvino and Valter help the family work the fields. Valter completes his compulsory schooling.

1955

Forced to leave his farming job, Guerrino Scavolini uses his severance package to open a coffee bar/grocery store in Pesaro.

1956

Elvino and Valter Scavolini are hired by Gorini, a small Pesaro company in the home-furnishing industry undergoing strong expansion at the time. Elvino is a machinery operator, Valter does assembly and painting. The first Pesaro furniture fair opens—biennial until '66; annual thereafter—to promote local companies that have evolved over the previous decade from artisanal to industrial operations, including Fastigi, Bacchiani, Tonelli, Cartoceti and Nicolini. In subsequent years, Scavolini would regularly exhibit at the Pesaro trade show (eventually known as SAMP).

1960

Elvino Scavolini marries Carolina Bassi in April. They will have four children: Emanuela (1961), Tiziana (1964), Alberto (1969) and Elena (1975).

1961

Valter Scavolini decides to leave Gorini and start his own business. After much debate, his father, reluctant at first (he wanted his sons to follow him in the retail business), made 19-year-old Valter a loan of 400,000 lire (about 3000 euros, adjusted for inflation) for his business venture. The father insists on the presence of a partner, Alfio Vitali, a friend and peer of Valter, who remained by his side until 1967. Acquiring the necessary woodworking equipment with promissory notes and leasing a shed in Santa Veneranda, a farming village outside Pesaro where the family lived, Valter's business starts up a modest production of kitchen furniture, sideboards, buffets and sideboards, still on the artisanal scale. The work is exhausting and unhealthy, largely because of the vapors from the lacquering process. The hours, too, are extreme: three shifts per day (7 to noon; 2 to 7pm; 8 to midnight), sometimes including Saturday and Sunday. Elvino, who works evenings from the beginning, takes on more responsibility to help his brother.

1962

Elvino Scavolini leaves Gorini and joins Valter. Edmondo Nobili is hired as an accountant by the fledgling company. A rigorous and capable man, Nobili would assume increasingly important roles and responsibilities as the company's revenues grew. The first machines for working plastic laminates are introduced to the production line. Having carefully assessed the market, Scavolini begins focusing on modular kitchens. The first such model is Svedese, faced in plastic laminate in cherry and walnut finishes.

Edmondo Nobili

I was the first employee hired by the company in April 1962, mostly for accounting duties. At the end of the '60s I became CEO, though I didn't have anything to do with product

Edmondo Nobili, 2006

development or production. There are a number of reasons, I think, for the success of our group. First and foremost, the intelligence, dedication and enterprising spirit of the Scavolini brothers—Valter was already a brilliant talent when I met him at the age of 20, while Elvino was always confident and reliable. Both devoted themselves entirely to the company. I should also emphasize the high quality of our products, our absolutely competitive prices—thanks to our control of the supply chain—our high productivity, and the absence of financial debts which would have raised costs. Other key factors were the constant attention to all the commercial sectors and to product design, the insistence on conducting training courses for employees and dealers, and the continuous investment of significant resources in advertising. Then there was our special relationship with the dealers, to whom we always provided reliable service, particularly in managing orders, deliveries and post-sales assistance. Along with all of this, another central factor was a certain professional deontology that I wouldn't hesitate to call 'Calvinist' (given that I consider myself as such, and have always championed its values). By this I mean seriousness in all personal and professional relationships, absolute rigor in terms of payment deadlines, immediate invoicing and, consequently, updated accounting. What does this mean? Well, for one thing it means selling only through the dealer network and not directly to the end-user. We have never indulged in direct sales or discounts for friends—our prices and conditions are the same for everyone without exception, and in this we are and always have been very 'German'. This is what I mean by rigor in the business world. It should also be noted that even before the advent of the

computer, our administrative processes had always been rational. And then when information technology arrived in the 1970s, we were among the first in Italy to use it. We have always planned our investments step by step, looking forward, but with our feet firmly on the ground. When we decentralized production through a network of subcontractors, all Italian, that turned out to be fundamental to our growth. I should point out that Valter and Elvino always believed in the severe application of rules because they saw it as a driver of mental flexibility and entrepreneurial spirit, never as rigidity as an end in itself. There are so many things I could recount, of course.... One thing I can say is that over the course of my career I was involved to some extent in everything, from the selection of collaborators to arranging cultural and sports sponsorships, from working in direct contact with the complex network of dealers and agents to giving names to the models—though that was only at the beginning. To give just one example, Selquy, a deliberately economical kitchen from 1976, takes its name from the initials of a famous Italian statesman, Quintino Sella, because the model reminded me of a well-known expression of his, "economical to the bone." Obviously I did all of this in close collaboration with the brothers—Elvino, a singular man when it came to relationships, capable of creating that balanced atmosphere that encouraged people to work together to obtain the best results; and Valter, always busy and enterprising, a true entrepreneur. I tried many times to get him to stop and reflect a moment, but once he latched onto an idea it was difficult to stop him! It really was a great adventure, I have to say, full of personal satisfaction, exemplary from a human perspective. I was lucky to have been able to dedicate almost 50 years of living and working to

Valter Scavolini,
Edmondo Nobili and
Elvino Scavolini, 1996

Elvino Scavolini and
Carolina Bassi at the time
of their engagement,
1959

Scavolini, a long and happy period, thanks in part to all the people I worked with, all of us sharing the principles of reciprocal respect and esteem—the same that characterized my relationship with the second generation of Scavolinis when they joined the company.
CEO of Scavolini from the 1960s to 2003

1963
Finest and Italia join Svedese, bringing the number of initial Scavolini models to three.

Michela Acanfora
Sometime in the first half of the 1960s, the Scavolini brothers, who had only just launched their business, took part in a trade fair in Naples. Valter was introduced to us by a salesman, but we knew practically nothing about them except through a rather limited 'catalogue' that had been sent to our store. We liked him immediately for the spirit of determination he conveyed. When the fair was over, my husband, a serious cabinetmaker, decided to take the train to Pesaro to see how their factory was organized and to follow the various phases of production. Such an affinity was established there that our friendship continues to this day. We used to tell Valter that he had to advertise, because people would come into the store asking for Salvarani. He listened, but always said "Let me work out the kinks first, then I'll advertise." Well, I think it's safe to say that he eventually listened to us! I remember that we were always complaining about the tables, which were too small. Here in Naples, families are large, five or six kids was the norm. We tried to figure out how to accommodate them. And I remember Elvino, who would secretly pass us packages of assorted hardware, like a grandfather filling his grandchildren's pockets with candy.

The trade shows were always a lot of fun back then. We used to bring five or six sold orders to make a good impression, the kind of thing that today would be seen as naive. With Valter and Elvino, every trade show was an occasion for getting together, partying, revelry. Valter and my husband would play *bocce*, there was a real family atmosphere. As Scavolini grew, things of course started to change. Everything became more professional, which is how it should be. However, I must confess that I'm a little sorry. I remember that our customers at the beginning were much, much easier to manage. Lacking any specific knowledge of materials and possible solutions, they entrusted everything to us. They would show us the room we had to furnish, then we took care of everything. And they never gave us any trouble, in part for the reasons I mentioned, but also because we were very professional. In terms of sales, the first success was the Italia model, the third kitchen in Scavolini's product line, then Flower, Connye, l'Isola della Melarosa and, more recently, Carol. But the all-time number one was Color, an innovative model that we installed in practically every home in our area. The customers of today, on the other hand…. I think it's clear that the future will give way more and more to technology—unfortunately, I must say. The kitchen shouldn't be anything more than a comfortable place to work, that's all. What else should it be?
Owner of Scavolini dealer Mobili Casillo in Naples and head of a family active in the furnishing business since 1947

1965
Valter Scavolini marries Marisa Bassi, sister of Elvino's wife Carolina, which tightens yet further the already strong family bonds. Like Elvino, he has four children: Gian Marco (1966), Barbara (1968), Fabiana (1970) and Andrea

Valter Scavolini and
Marisa Bassi at the time
of their engagement,
1963

(1979). The company moves to a more spacious and comfortable facility in Pesaro. For the first time, the sales representatives are equipped with the first real Scavolini catalogue.

1967

Definitive relocation to the new facility in Montelabbate, about 8 miles outside Pesaro in the direction of Urbino, soon to become one of the most important industrial zones in the province. Scavolini assumes a corporate structure, graduating from micro-business to industrial enterprise with a national sales network. The official name becomes 'Mobilificio F.lli Scavolini snc'. The production plant, originally with an area of around 8,400 square feet (later to be expanded many times over), accommodates 20 or so employees. The production line takes on a colorful note with Flower, a model built in hollow-core with chrome yellow and sand laminate facing, and with handles and strips in walnut-tinted laminate. At this point, Scavolini had already begun offering customers a wide range of appliances.

1968

Scavolini gets its first logo: an 'S' wrapped in a banderole, the style

decidedly Pop. The color is red, which symbolizes the company and is the same as the current logo.

1969

This is the year of Color, one of the most successful models in Scavolini's history. Built in hollow-core faced with walnut laminate, its distinguishing feature is a reversible central panel framed by solid wood.

1973

The era of sports sponsorship begins with the Muraglia football club, named for a district of Pesaro.

1974

Scavolini exhibits at Eurocucina, a biennial international trade fair that opened this year in Milan. Scavolini would never miss a year from 1978 on.

1975

The company launches a national print and television campaign (expanded in 1984 to the private networks). A cartoon character called *Il Cuochino*, a fat and friendly little chef who gives cooking lessons, is adopted to accompany the slogan "*Scavolini la cucina con ottimi ingredienti*" (or 'Scavolini, the kitchen with excellent ingredients', which plays

Pesaro's Muraglia football
team, 1973

on the double meaning of *cucina,* which also translates as 'cuisine'). The company expands its role as sport sponsor with Scavolini Basket Pesaro. Agostino Bertani is the first outside designer to work for the company—up to this point, all models had been designed in-house by Studio Vuesse (the Italian phoneticisation of 'VS', Valter Scavolini's initials). Among Bertani's contributions are Connye, a big seller that evokes "the warmth of tradition" and marks the beginning of a whole line of retro kitchens, and the Isola della Melarosa model. This latter, characterized by "soft and sober lines", is built in hollow-core with daffodil white laminate and doors in various colors (white, beige, clivia red, monsoon grey as well as natural tints like ash and mahogany), with an aluminum baseboard that appears to lift the unit from the floor. Scavolini reaches 3 billion lire in revenues (approx. 1.5 million euros, not adjusted for inflation).

1978

Dante Benini designs two models with hollow-core structures, Happy and Merry. The first has solid pine doors, the second comes in different colors and conveys "an elegant and modern image." Simone Donato creates L'Elite, a model distinguished by the linear interlocking of the components.

1979

Scavolini issues stock and becomes a publicly traded company.

1980

Emanuela Scavolini, daughter of Elvino, joins the company. After an apprenticeship of about six years in the sales office, she begins working on external relations and human resources (later also in the Fondazione Scavolini instituted in 1984).
Scavolini becomes the sponsor of the city of Pesaro baseball team.

1981

Scavolini becomes the sponsor of the city of Aquila's rugby team.

1982

Scavolini becomes official sponsor to the Rossini Opera Festival (ROF), an event organized by the city of Pesaro since 1980 in honor of the musical genius of native son Gioachino Rossini and to spread awareness of his work.
Scavolini Aquila Rugby wins its fourth league championship.
Simone Donato designs Fanny, a model in antiqued birch "whose line remains deeply tied to the healthiest traditions. The presence of a breadbox, sideboard and bench further accentuate this aspect." Enrico Tonucci designs Trapezio, a model that "breaks free of the schemes of the traditional kitchen" through the emphasis given to the structural elements of the beechwood frame "and is suited to younger tastes and to spaces like rented efficiency apartments and studios."

Valter Scavolini, Adriano
and Claudio Panatta,
1983

Valter Scavolini
celebrates with the
Pesaro basketball team
after winning the 1983
Cup Winners Cup

Right
The Isabel kitchen (Studio
Vuesse, 1985) provides
a backdrop for the Pesaro
basketball team, 1985

1983

Pesaro native Massimo Dolcini, one of
the leading Italian graphic designers of
his generation, begins working with
Scavolini. A protégé in Urbino of Albe
Steiner and Michele Provinciali and later
a professor himself, Dolcini and the
studios under his purview (Fuorischema,
M&M, Dolcini Associati) imprint a
powerful identity on the company's mode
of communication. Dolcini's work also
extends into activities where Scavolini is
present as a sponsor, as in the case of the
ROF and various publishing initiatives.
Scavolini also begins collaborating with
Studio 33, a Pesaro-based industrial
photography agency run by Mauro
Tamburini, which continues to this day.
The number of new models increases,
encompassing diverse design
philosophies and furnishing solutions.
Pierluigi Molinari designs Cabriolet,
notable for its geometric rigor and sliding
doors, while Studio Vuesse proposes
Dolly, a kitchen in oak that celebrates
the artisanal qualities typical of Italian
production, because "the hectic and often
exhausting pace of modern life drives
taste toward reassuring forms that
express traditional values not yet lost."

Studio Vuesse also designs Fiordaliso,
"fresh and lovely as a flower."

1984

Scavolini's revenues make it the number
one Italian manufacturer of modular
kitchens, a primacy that it maintains
today. In order to translate its sense of
rootedness in the Pesaro area into
concrete action, the Fondazione Scavolini
is created on July 30th. Its offices are in
Villa Montani in Ginestreto, a patrician
residence built in various phases between
the 16th and 19th centuries, which was
bought up by the Scavolini family in
1985. The four-year restoration project
was overseen by Celio Francioni
(architecture) and Roberta Martufi
(landscaping). Among the Foundation's
missions are the promotion of projects
and initiatives of a cultural, artistic and
educational nature, the realization of
projects and initiatives aimed at
improving the conservation of the region's
cultural heritage, and the financing and
publishing of studies of significant
historical, artistic, archaeological and
ethno-anthropological interest. The
Foundation, whose direction would be
entrusted to Emanuela Scavolini in 1994,

Above, from left
Marisa and Valter, Elvino
and Carolina, Guerrino
Scavolini, 1984

Below, from left
Tiziana, Alberto, Gian
Marco, Fabiana, Elena,
Barbara, Andrea,
Emanuela and, in the
center, grandfather
Guerrino Scavolini, 1984

also publishes two ongoing series of
periodicals, *Quaderni* (12 issues as of
2010) and *Catasti* (3 issues). Current
activities are concentrated on the recovery
and restoration of artifacts ignored by
institutions. Raffaella Carrà, the most
popular entertainer of the moment, is
invited by Valter Scavolini to become the
face that represents the company to the
public. The slogan "Scavolini, Italy's
favorite kitchen" is launched and becomes
famous. The first of a successful series of
spots for the new advertising campaign is
filmed at Cinecittà, in "a large theatre
expressly equipped for cinematic
productions, with creative and technical
personnel who ordinarily work in cinema."
Supported by a comprehensive print,
radio and television (public and private)
advertising campaign, a kitchen designed
by Studio Vuesse and named for the new
public representative, Raffaella, is
launched. Lacquered to a gloss, with
countertops in granite, laminate or
Carrara marble, it rides the wave of the
ad campaign and becomes the symbol of
an era, "truly a dream kitchen." This is
also the year of Emily, which revisits the
overall configuration and details of Happy
(1978), and of Gardenia, "dedicated above

all to young people who like to move with
total freedom in their homes."

1986
A new advert filmed at Cinecittà with
Raffaella Carrà: "A jet displaying the
Scavolini logo has just landed. Raffaella
descends, radiant and regal, greeted by
an excited crowd of photographers,
journalists, fans and curious onlookers."
The minimal and compact Dandy is
introduced, with the option of suspended
shelves and graphic definition (in wood
or colors) in the alternation of doors,
shelves and drawers. Its practical
simplicity is widely appreciated and
Dandy becomes one of the best-selling
models in the company's history.

1987
Lorella Cuccarini replaces Raffaella Carrà
as the face that represented the company
to the public, a role she would maintain
until 2004. She becomes the 'face' of
Scavolini, embodying its family values—
young and energetic, while at the same
time serious and reliable. The integration
between the company and popular
soubrette, who inherits the title of "The
best seller from Italy", is total, and serves

Scavolini technical office,
second half of the 1980s

Promotional postcards
announcing the summer
closure of the plant,
1984–87

Presentation page of the
Camelia model (Studio
Vuesse, 1986) from the
Scavolini catalogue

Page from the in-house
graphic identity manual
(*Manuale di
identificazione grafica
Scavolini*), 1991

Scavolini sales point
in Larissa, Greece

as the basis for a long-term television and print ad campaign. Silvano Barsacchi designs Lorella in her honor, a sleek and practical kitchen. Scavolini's expansion into foreign markets begins when Anastasios Exarchos opens the first showroom outside of Italy in Larissa, Greece.

Anastasios Exarchos

Right from the very beginning I felt like a part of the big Scavolini family, as did my own wife and two children. The story begins in 1987. With my degree in pharmacology from the University of Bologna, I ran a pharmacy back home in Greece. But my passion for Italy drove me to seek out a business contact with the country where I'd studied. At the time I was working as a translator for a used-car dealer and I asked him to find an Italian kitchen manufacturer with whom I could collaborate—my wife was already in the kitchen business. He gave me a Scavolini catalogue, saying, "They are the best. If you can get them, you'll have a lot of work." So I went with a former associate to Pesaro and asked very simply if I could be their representative in Greece (Scavolini had negligible sales in my country at the time). They granted us rights to sell their products for one year, to test our abilities and professionalism. We ordered and received the first kitchens just before Christmas 1987 (I still remember the models: Raffaella, Dandy, Fiordaliso, and there was also a Jenny), everything delivered to Larissa to the store I had there, and still have. We were one of the first kitchen brands in Greece. It was great. People would enter the store, attracted by the Italian design and the Scavolini name, which was well-known as a basketball sponsor. But then they'd ask the price and walk out laughing, for they were ten times higher than the price of local kitchens. Initially it was very difficult. We had to work hard to inform clients about the brand, help them see the

differences and the quality of Scavolini kitchens, insist obviously on the virtues of 'Made in Italy'. And things went well—in fact, I left the pharmacy. I then opened two stores for direct sales in Katerini and Iraklion (Crete), and many others as an agent. The people at Scavolini were always available and ready to help, though I should stress the invaluable assistance of Edmondo Nobili, who did everything to ensure the success of our enterprise. And I cannot forget Elvino Scavolini, who needed only a few words to find a solution to every problem we encountered, he was a rock for us. I'm sure we'll be working with Scavolini for many, many years to come, if only for the fact that through this brand I was able to make my great desire—or rather, dream—come true: of being in constant contact with Italy, to represent Italian design in my country, and to find a company—in this case a family, too—that is serious, highly organized, stable and ethically unimpeachable. For me, Valter Scavolini is a beacon. It's no accident that he is at the top in his field, or that Scavolini is not only Italy's favorite kitchen, but probably Greece's as well. In my country, this brand is a benchmark not only for design and product quality, but also for the absolute punctuality of deliveries, the consistency of the advertising, the effort put into the creation of exclusive points of sale. I have total faith in the future: Valter Scavolini will do his best not only for himself but for all of us, I'm sure of it, with the support of his family's second generation and by all his collaborators, all of whom work devotedly for the group. I, too, have my sons working alongside me, Andreas and Vaggelis. Family support, not only from the Scavolini family but from my own, has been fundamental for me. I would like to thank them, and all the dealers in Greece who believe as I do in this mission.
Director of Thema, agent and dealer for Scavolini in Greece since 1987

The Scavolini Basket Pesaro team, 1990; promotional postcard for a television sponsorship tied to the 1990 World Cup

1988

The basketball team from Pesaro sponsored by Scavolini wins its first season title. Valter and Elvino Scavolini decide to celebrate the victory with a colossal 'maxi-banquet' along the Pesaro seashore that involves the entire population of the city and remains for several years in the Guinness Book of World Records. Roberto Ciolli designs Donna Rosa, a retro kitchen in wood with bronzed fixtures.

1989

The company approaches 150 billion lire in sales (approx. 77 million euros). The Fondazione Scavolini opens a museum in the birthplace of the great composer Gioachino Rossini. Alison and Honey, both designed by Silvano Barsacchi, signal a return to the theme of minimalist sobriety that would become widespread in the following decade.

1990

Scavolini Basket Pesaro wins its second championship. New advertising campaign with Lorella Cuccarini providing the testimonial. Silvano Barsacchi designs Blondie and Lietta, apparently reflecting on the expressive possibilities of a luxury that does not yet want to surrender to minimalist reduction.

Promotional postcards commemorating the record-breaking 'victory table' along Pesaro coast for the first ever league title of the local basketball team (1988) and the sponsorship of the 10th Rossini Opera Festival (1989)

The identification of Lorella Cuccarini with Scavolini left its mark on the recent history of advertising in Italy
Above
Images from the 1987 advertising campaign

Below
1999 advertising campaign, Baltimora kitchen (Studio Vuesse with Marco Pareschi, 1999)

Lorella Cuccarini

"For every model we did a different spot, some of which were veritable films. I remember one episode during the second year of my contract when we spent about ten days at Cinecittà," recalls Lorella Cuccarini. "The crew we were working with was fantastic, a big group of people all working in harmony. The late '80s and early '90s were the golden years. We would average one spot a year, though sometimes we'd shoot several together for a campaign designed to run a couple of years or so. It was a special adventure right from the outset. My relationship with the Scavolini family was professional, of course, but it was also much more. I always felt at home with them. There was the Pesaro furniture fair, so for many years I went to the presentation of the new models. We shared a lot of great moments together, like the basketball championship won by the Scavolini-sponsored team…memories one doesn't forget. I worked for them for 17 years, which speaks for itself. When they originally asked me to be their public face, I was shocked!

This was 1987, when I was between gigs—the second season of *Fantastico*, the TV show I was doing with Pippo Baudo, and the Festival of San Remo. The fact that Scavolini had chosen me to replace Raffaella Carrà was like a dream, I simply couldn't believe it. At that point, I hadn't ever done any advertising work apart from a brief stint with a stocking company. Scavolini's offer was for me a sign that something was really happening, that success had truly arrived. To take the place of Raffaella Carrà…I needed some time to gather my thoughts, I was only 20 years old. I think they chose me because of the spontaneity and freshness I managed to convey in the shows I'd been doing. Every ad shoot was a lot of fun because each one was a little story built around my character, like me coming home after a day at work and finally being able to relax in my personal space. The intention was to show the difference between the famous TV personality and the real Lorella, who goes home like everyone else and is happy to be in her private world. All the episodes we did were based

Una Scavolini è autentica ...come te

Cucina Baltimora design Vuesse con la collaborazione di Marco Pareschi

2003 advertising
campaign, Life kitchen
(Studio Vuesse, 2003)

on this premise, like little stories.
In terms of image and career, this thing
of being "*la più amata dagli italiani*"
(or, 'The best seller from Italy', with the
double meaning of Scavolini kitchens
and me) was positive overall.
Obviously, as with all successful
slogans—and this was about as
successful as they come—there's the
risk of being obscured. The key for me
was to not take it too seriously, to make
light of it all the many times that
people would refer to it or make jokes.
I would say, 'Hey, it's not me that the
Italians love so much, it's the kitchen!'
That was unavoidable. If it weren't for
Scavolini, this slogan probably never

would have existed. But today I'm no
longer that girl of twenty years ago, the
hypothetically ideal young bride.
I'm what I am, a woman with a
beautiful family and four children.
In the last spots I did with Scavolini,
this was the theme. In fact I have a
great relationship with my kitchen,
I inhabit it in a complete and vital
way. I'm the kind of person who loves
spending my free time cooking.
I have a living room that barely gets
used. Where do you think I help my
kids with their homework? At the
kitchen table, naturally".
*Testimonial Scavolini from 1987
to 2004*

Design Roberto Ciolli

Ortensia

Solidità, accoglienza, tecnologia e funzionalità sono i giusti requisiti di una cucina dei nostri giorni. Se a queste qualità si aggiunge la memoria di passate tradizioni, aumenterà il piacere di ritrovarsi nell'ambiente considerato a tutt'oggi il più importante della casa. Ortensia, la cucina in legno che illustriamo in queste pagine, è solida e capiente, affidabile in ogni occasione. Generosa nell'accogliere amici e familiari con selezioni tutte decisamente confortevoli, pronta in qualsiasi momento a soddisfare ogni più piccola necessità. Gli elementi piattaoio lavawii, che cominciano si taytiono alla tradizione, sono mobili, diversi per dimensioni e altezze, ciascuno destinato a una specifica funzione. Numerosi sono anche gli accessori e gli elettrodomestici. Tra i dettagli più ricercati: i pomelli in ceramica, i coverimani, i vetri lavorati trasparenti o gli originali e manicuiiti piani in gres che possono essere scelti in alternativa ai piani in laminato, marmo e granito comunque disponibili.

Presentation page of the Ortensia model (Roberto Ciolli, 1990) from the Scavolini catalogue

Promotional postcard announcing the summer closure of the plant, 1990. Promotional postcard for the 31st Pesaro Furniture Fair (SAMP), 1991

1991

Gian Marco Scavolini, Valter's son, joins the company and is initially assigned to work with the director of production, particularly with regard to quality control. Vittorio Renzi is hired and soon becomes head of the Italian sales office and begins handling marketing duties as well. Scavolini sponsors the Festival of San Remo and the television shows *Piacere Raiuno* and, through a contest, *L'amore è un albero verde*. The Scavolini advertising campaign, though still featuring the fixed presence of Lorella Cuccarini, is focused more directly on the presentation of the product. De Pas, D'Urbino and Lomazzi, historic names in Italian design, present Gemma, a model characterized by the contrast between linear and rounded forms. Lucci and Orlandini design the Mimsy kitchen. Beatrice, designed by Roberto Ciolli (who had anticipated its style the year before with Melissa and Ortensia), is the full and proud expression of a classical sensibility rooted in a specific market sector, both in Italy and abroad: "modeled on the tradition of a polished Venetian style, the doors are in cream colored oak with solid wood frames and veneered central panels. The knobs are in ceramic, with a little decoration in the middle." Silvano Barsacchi designs Fiandra, a kitchen with colored wood panels (greens, grays, reds) and metal handles.

Gian Marco Scavolini

I joined the company in 1991. I immediately dove in with intense passion and seriousness, proud to be part of this world and this family, taking inspiration every day from the example of my father and uncle. I began working with the director of production, Giovanni Severi, with particular focus on the area of quality control, learning a lot as I went. In 1992–93 Severi and I participated in a course on quality that was very instructive and that opened new prospects for us. During these years, our organization of quality was simpler than it is today, however there must have been a sort of intuitive complicity in our vision, for we both considered this aspect as a priority from the very beginning. It was an experience that stimulated me to commit myself completely to the issue, more determined than ever to embrace the company philosophy which I already felt I shared. We immediately understood that building a quality management system would be a big help to us. The target was the new international norms UNI EN ISO 9001 (then called 29001). After the implementation phase, we obtained certification in 1996, which has been confirmed every year since. It gave me true satisfaction, I must admit, one that rewarded our original intuition and confirmed that we had chosen the right path. A quality management system could be defined in simple terms as the optimization of the various company processes in accordance with a virtuous circle of improvement (known as the 'Deming cycle'), all aimed at

Promotional postcard for the official sponsorship of the San Remo Festival, 1991

Official recognition of Valter Scavolini as a Cavaliere del Lavoro, 1993

satisfying the customer. For example, in our case, the processes most involved are: product design and development, customer order management, the selection/evaluation/monitoring of suppliers, production and maintenance, inspection of materials and finished products in the incoming, production and outgoing phases, document management, complaint management. At a certain point, however, all of this was no longer enough because we had begun to think in different terms and with greater awareness of the environmental issue, because this too is an important part of the process of optimizing quality. The world population is growing, this is unavoidable. And given that one cannot slow down progress, the only solution left to us is to make sure that it's sustainable. I do not think by any means that the commitment to sustainability is a passing phenomenon. In the near future it will be the norm, and much less of a fad than it might, in certain ways, seem today. We were and still are deeply convinced that respect for nature is a duty, a necessity that we at Scavolini have always considered paramount—in the past, through simple actions tied to our immediate surroundings, today with operations of a broader scope and effectiveness. Translating these intentions into concrete action without compromising production is neither simple nor easy. But our commitment in this regard is total. Which is why, in the early 2000s when they were developing the first environmental management systems, we immediately understood the importance of the improvement that the implementation of the new international norms could bring, specifically UNI EN ISO 14001. After completing the work, we obtained certification in 2004. Then in 2009 we launched Scavolini Green Mind, an

ecosustainable project that runs throughout the entire production chain all the way to the finished product, focusing on the responsible use of resources, renewable energy, the recovery of waste materials. I strongly believe in Scavolini Green Mind, which gives us great satisfaction. When I heard a few months ago that the reforestation of the first 12 acres had been completed (to compensate for the energy we consumed in 2009), I was more convinced than ever that the path we have undertaken is truly the right one.

Director of Quality and Environment at Scavolini

1992

Restoration of the 15th-century devotional frescoes in the Romanesque parish church in the village of Ginestreto, part of the town of Montelabbate (Fondazione Scavolini). Giuliano Cappelletti and Enzo Pozzoli begin their design partnership with Scavolini with Petunia, a model in wood with colored inserts.

1993

Valter Scavolini is granted the title of Knight of Labor by the Italian State. Alberto Scavolini, Elvino's son, joins the company and is assigned to the function of coordinating communications. Launch of the Scavolini quality system, run by Gian Marco Scavolini. To celebrate the company's first three decades, a volume is published entitled *1962–1992. Trent'anni di cucine Scavolini*. Produced by the public relations office, it contains texts by Marta Alessandri and Franco Panzini, with graphic design by Dolcini Associati (Leonardo Sonnoli, Antonio Trebbi). In the presentation, Valter and Elvino Scavolini state that "at the conclusion of this publishing project, we can assert with greater clarity the extent to which

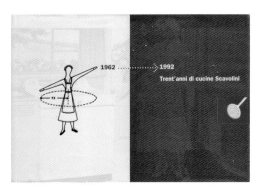

The book published to celebrate the first three decades of Scavolini's history, designed by Dolcini Associati

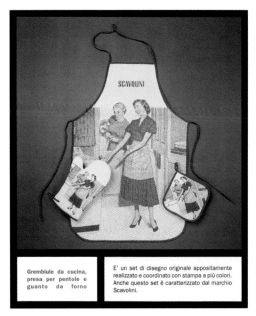

Grembiule da cucina, presa per pentole e guanto da forno

E' un set di disegno originale appositamente realizzato e coordinato con stampa a più colori. Anche questo set è caratterizzato dal marchio Scavolini.

Set including apron, oven mitt and pot holder, 1994

Scavolini has expressed the evolution of the taste of the average Italian family over the years. We therefore feel that we can proudly claim to have conquered a place, albeit small, in our country's history." The first design by Gianni Pareschi for Scavolini, the Country model, is introduced.

Alberto Scavolini

I joined the company in 1993, initially working in communications. I spent my first few years ferreting out the secrets of the profession, working alongside the technicians and above all absorbing everything I could from my Uncle Valter. He has a pure business talent, and I don't say this as his nephew, but as someone who has had the fortune to work with him and truly understand, day after day, how to work seriously in this field. I have wonderful memories, which I treasure, of the unique relationship between my father and uncle. I remember that they would often talk in the doorway that connected their offices, always in dialect. Dense, intense conversations. My father was the solid pillar of the company, the one with his feet on the ground, the 'hardware' of Scavolini. Uncle Valter is instead the 'software', the man with a million ideas, always looking ahead. My father was a man of few words, but when he spoke Valter listened to him attentively. These may seem like normal features of a relationship between brothers, but they had a truly special bond that was fundamentally important for the functioning of the Scavolini machine. Then, in 2003, the moment arrived for me to take a big step. Vittorio Renzi had left the directorship of Ernestomeda to take that same job at Scavolini, so, quite simply, an important position opened up. The family had started talking about the situation. We have never precluded

capable people, as the choice of Renzi demonstrates, nor have we ever thought that the Scavolini surname was an automatic ticket for privilege. I remember my cousin Fabiana openly asking, "What if one of us were to take the job?" Uncle Valter thought about it and asked us cousins if anyone was interested. I thought about it a while and presented my candidacy. Which was accepted. I have to admit that it was a rather intense moment. I was only 34 and I wondered if I hadn't taken too big a step, a crazy leap even. On the one hand there was my uncle, who supported me and reassured me that everything would be fine, that he would personally help me, to not be afraid. On the other there was my father: "Are you sure? You know that this is a very big responsibility, a great, even exhausting weight...". He wasn't saying this to stop me, but to make sure I knew exactly what the reality was, which he was very well aware of. But it all worked out. Ernestomeda is a great company, with a lively structure and lots of stimuli. There are 110 of us altogether, we all know each other. We have a distribution network of about 350 dealers, including 15 mono-brand flagship stores in some of the major Italian and international capitals— Lugano, Chicago, Los Angeles, Seoul, Madrid, Barcelona, Beirut, Milan. We also have a special section for the detailed study of kitchens for yachts, mega-yachts and cruise ships, Ernestomeda Yacht Division. Our production is geared toward quality contemporary design. We work with some of the best designers in the world—Pietro Arosio, Carlo Bartoli, Castiglia Associati, Rodolfo Dordoni, Zaha Hadid, Jean Nouvel, Marc Sadler—and this of course is a great satisfaction both for us and our customers. Ernestomeda is a company unto itself, though tied to

Pictures of two
workshops organized by
Scavolini in 1994 and
2010

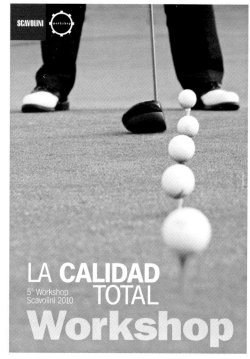

The Ernestomeda factory
in Montelabbate

Scavolini. Our production facilities
are adjoined, our products are different,
but we share the same fundamental
spirit of professionalism and
dedication to our work.
CEO, Ernestomeda

1994

The "Insieme per crescere" project is
launched ('Growing Together'), a cycle
of workshops for Scavolini dealers that
investigate issues regarding sales
techniques, communications, accounting
management and marketing in relation
to the changes in the market.
The Fondazione Scavolini restores two
important 14th-century marble portals
for the churches of San Francesco
(1994) and San Domenico (2000), both
in Pesaro. From this year forward, the
Foundation participates in the Rossini
Opera Festival as a promoter.

1995

Fabiana Scavolini, Valter's daughter,
joins the company as assistant to the
marketing director. The Flamek brand
is born, targeted at customers looking

for simple, economical, high-quality
products. The successful march of
another new brand, Ernestomeda,
begins with the acquisition (December
6th) of a kitchen manufacturing plant
in Montelabbate and all its equipment.
Targeted at the upper-middle and high
end of the market, Ernestomeda
proposes top of the design range
products at competitive prices.
The Fondazone Scavolini restores the
18th-century chapel of the Beato Sante,
located in the sanctuary of the same
name in the town of Mombaroccio.

1996

By encompassing all the company's
brands, the Scavolini Group is formed
to better respond to the diversification
that the market demands in growing
measure. It is a move that facilitates
the exploitation of the enormous
advantages of economy of scale. Launch
of Ernestomeda, which clocks in at the
end of the year with revenues of more
than 4 million euros. Scavolini is among
the first companies in Italy to obtain
the UNI EN ISO 9001 certification for

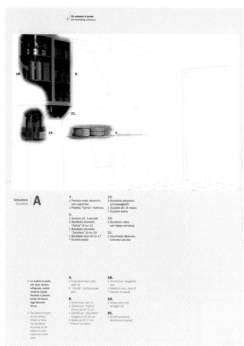

Above, from left
Pages from the Scavolini
publication, *L'arredo
giusto per le nostre
cucine*, 1996

Right
Three promotional
postcards, 1996

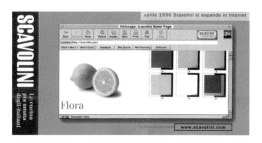

The Scavolini website in
1996 and 2005

quality management, which has been confirmed every year since. The website scavolini.com goes online, establishing direct, interactive contact between the company and its customers. Raffaello Pravato designs Domobel, a traditional kitchen in black walnut.

1997

Vittorio Renzi becomes CEO of Ernestomeda. The Komma agency of Milan begins working on Scavolini's advertising and communications. The relationship, which began with the launch of Ernestomeda, will endure over the years to come. The Fondazione begins work on the recovery of a wing of the 18th-century convent of San Giovanni Battista in Pesaro, with the aim of converting it into the city's main public library (1997–99).

1999

Silvano Barsacchi designs Tess, a model whose crisp volumes anticipate the taste of the new millennium. Darling, by Raffaello Pravato, is instead a traditional kitchen built with the attention to detail one would expect

from an artisan. It features doors in Italian walnut, carved baseboards and a range of accessories that evoke the atmosphere of days gone by. In collaboration with Marco Pareschi, Studio Vuesse creates Baltimora, a model destined to enjoy many years of success.

2000

Fabiana Scavolini becomes director of marketing and sales for Italy. Scavolini begins planning Utility System—a project by Renzo Baldanello and Bernardino Pittino, winners of a 1998 competition sponsored by the Fondazione Don Gaudiano of Pesaro— which should ideally transform any and every model into an accessible, barrier-free space for senior citizens and people with disabilities or limited motor capacity. The Fondazione conducts a comprehensive restoration of the historic Jewish cemetery of the city of Pesaro (2000–02).

Fabiana Scavolini
Being the daughter of a businessman who has accomplished extraordinary

Promotional postcard for
the 1997–98 basketball
season

Scavolini basketball 97, 98

U.S. Victoria Libertas Pallacanestro s.s.p.a.

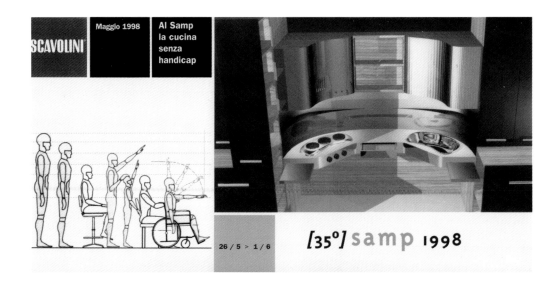

things gives one a great sense of responsibility. It's a valuable heritage, for sure, but also extremely demanding. Fortunately, this heritage is divided by four, insofar as my brother Gian Marco and our cousins Emanuela and Alberto also work with the company. My father and uncle built a kitchen manufacturing business that in 1984 became number one in Italy, *"la più amata dagli italiani."* When I hear about what they accomplished, about how much they were and are respected and loved, I feel 'small' next to them and wonder how I could ever achieve their stature. The most logical way, I tell myself, is to follow their example and their teachings. My father and Uncle Elvino were always driven by the

same principles: first and foremost the family, then work, respect for the context in which the company operates (i.e., Scavolini's commitment to local sports teams, the Rossini Opera Festival and Fondazione Scavolini), respect for other people. But perhaps the most important lesson I learned from my father, and the trait of his that impresses me most, is the fact that he has always remained a simple man, devoted to the real values of life, to family, to lifelong friends, to the soil, and last but not least, to love for one's work. These might sound like clichés or advertising slogans if they weren't true. Still today my father is one of the first to arrive at the office and one of the last to leave. It is our duty, as the second

Scavolini generation, to perpetuate these values, always reminding ourselves, based on the example of my father and uncle, that our group consists first and foremost of men and women, people whom we count on, people who have helped us get to where we are and who will continue to accompany us on our journey. It is only by adhering to these principles that it becomes possible to work in a way that brings out the most in people, that ensures maximum involvement and consequently the best results. We are and will continue to be a unified, winning team. Moreover, we must always remember that in order to maintain these levels and aim ever higher, we need the maximum

commitment and constant dedication of everyone involved. Our communication should mirror our business ethic without falsity: a clean, consistent image that shows who we really are, our values and our commitment. No false promises or lofty rhetorical flights. Even the famous faces that represented Scavolini to the public, Raffaella Carrà and Lorella Cuccarini, were chosen not just for their fame but above all because they fit with our vision. As for the future, in order to best manage the difficulties that a family business eventually has to face, such as succession of ownership, we decided several years ago to make a family pact, based on the idea of safeguarding the company with intelligence and

reciprocal respect, and of keeping it clear that the company must come before everything and everyone's individual interests. The pact also regulates the eventual entry of new family members, such that any newcomer will join Scavolini with the full awareness, the same that we have, of being at the service of the group. In any case, the future of Scavolini will still be firmly in the hands of Valter Scavolini. He *is* the company, and all of us must take advantage of every opportunity to learn from his method and his intelligence. We will try to continue to approach the market informed and prepared, handling difficulties with faith and common sense like we've always done, with decisiveness when necessary. We will be ever more attentive to our customers and their needs, keeping in mind that our products are present in many different countries and cultures. Then, who knows, maybe one day we will broaden the confines of our famous slogan and Scavolini will become not just Italy's, but the world's favorite kitchen!

Director of Marketing and Sales for Scavolini Italy

2001

With the goal of presenting the world of Scavolini and its products in a faster, more dynamic and versatile language, one inspired by web culture and capable of creating a close contact with the customer, the new Scavolini catalogue, *Kitchens.it*, comes out in May. The format is that of a magazine, constantly updated and enriched by changing series of features and contributions.

2002

Gian Marco Scavolini takes over responsibility for the company's environmental program. Utility System goes into production. *Kitchens.it* debuts on the newsstand as a supplement to the main Italian design and furnishings magazines (4 million copies).
The web portal of the same name, www.kitchens.it, goes online in May.

2003

Edmondo Nobili retires and Vittorio Renzi replaces him as CEO of Scavolini. Alberto Scavolini becomes CEO of Ernestomeda. Scavolini Basic is born, a low-budget line that nonetheless maintains high formal standards, replacing Flamek. Revenues break the 150 million euro mark. A book celebrating more than 40 years of activity is published under the direction of the Komma agency. The tone and graphics are deliberately spare and minimal, without emphasis or exaggeration, in keeping with the company philosophy: "You are about to enter the world of Scavolini. We will try not to tell you the usual stories, but to help you better understand who we are. Welcome". Scavolini sponsors the women's volleyball team Robursport Pesaro. The kitchen program Happening (Studio Vuesse) proposes a new way of thinking about the space of the kitchen: subdivision of the food preparation areas, organization of storage volumes, greater freedom of movement. It comprises five models— Life, City, Dream, Home and Play— similar in form but with varying structures and colors (Bellagio cherry, white, aluminum grey, antique walnut, bleached oak).

Vittorio Renzi

I came to Scavolini in March 1991. Among my many memories is my meeting with the legendary Edmondo Nobili, then CEO, the Scavolini brothers' right-hand man since the beginning. I was more curious about the meeting than I was nervous or interested in the position, for I had just been offered a job with a bank. Nobili exerted a great fascination over me, presenting Scavolini like a big gym, a great opportunity for someone who wanted to really apply themselves. When Scavolini offered me the position, it was like a bolt of lightning on a sunny day and I found myself in a serious crisis. In the end, I decided to join them. With humility and hard work, I tried to make myself useful everywhere and to better understand my new surroundings before launching grand and reckless plans, as young college grads are often wont to do. Seen from the inside, the Scavolini 'machine' gradually revealed itself to me. Nothing especially sophisticated or secret; everything was instead very simple, conducted with a rare, almost miraculous discipline. And behind it all was the determination and the dream of the two brothers who had rolled up their sleeves and succeeded in turning their company into an example in terms of organization and communication. After the initial period of rising in the ranks, I became director of sales for Italy and also began taking on marketing responsibilities. These were difficult years—Italy was facing hard times, the modular kitchen market was suffering. We at Scavolini, after much research and discussion, decided to avoid wasting our energy and concentrate even more on what we knew how to do truly well. So we launched Flamek, a 'service' brand with affordable prices, simple (but still attractive) solutions and reduced modularity. We then moved on to tackle the high end of the market with an innovative gamble: we bought Nicolini Cucine, which had a great plant right across from ours in Montelabbate, and embarked on the adventure of a new brand, Ernestomeda. After a transitional phase, I was asked to become the CEO. I was still very young,

An image taken from the book published in 2003 to mark more than forty years of Scavolini's history

with a necessarily limited experience, so yes, I was terrified by the responsibility I was being asked to assume. However, not only was I reassured by the owners, but urged to accept the challenge, which began in March 1997. Thanks to the help of Scavolini and an excellent team of collaborators, Ernestomeda quickly became a success. This was an important signal for us. Except in rare cases, high-end design had never been the core business of Pesaro-based companies like ours for a number of reasons. With Ernestomeda we demonstrated the possibility of changing all that. This led us to start thinking that the parent company might be able to position itself at a higher level. And the rest is history, so to speak. In May 2003 I was asked to replace Edmondo Nobili, who was retiring, as CEO of Scavolini. Such an honor, and such responsibility. Ernestomeda was one thing, but Scavolini is another entirely, not only in terms of much, much larger numbers—employees, revenues—but also history and tradition. The job is mostly a matter of fine-tuning, trying to improve things that already functioned very well, but it also involves imagining significant changes in course. With me are Marco Signoretti, my second in command, and many other serious and reliable people with skills that can only be acquired by working in a leading company for years. The politics of the group has always prioritized the cultivation of enduring relationships founded on absolute transparency and rigor, accompanied by professional skills that are the envy of everyone. When I started as CEO, we immediately had to face a major internal reorganization—developing the first automated warehouse, the Assist project which overhauled the entire computer system, etc.—as well as a major change of course with regard to

our communication. After 20 years of promoting Scavolini through celebrities, it was to be the brand, by now extremely well-known to the Italian public, that would be the focus of a strategy based on clear and direct messages. This direction was also pursued in foreign markets through campaigns aimed at inserting our name into the exclusive circle of Italian brands known all over the world. On the product front, we replaced Flamek with Scavolini Basic, and completed our range of products for sophisticated, high-end customers. We acknowledged the catalyzing role that 'name' designers could have and thus created a series of mono-brand stores, which have proven to be fundamental in terms of both distribution and the communication of the brand. We accentuated all that, with a meticulousness that I wouldn't hesitate to call maniacal, through the consolidation of our physical presence on the market and a new and attentive development strategy on the international front (with the acquisition in 2008 of a prestigious space on West Broadway in New York, our first true American flagship store, we created Scavolini USA Inc.), and by participating in all the most important foreign trade shows. But now is not the time to rest on our laurels, though laurels are not lacking. In an increasingly open and globalized market, we have much more on the horizon than we do at our backs. We cannot simply sit around and tell each other how great we are, but must work as hard as our formidable predecessors did.
CEO, Scavolini

2004

Elvino Scavolini passes away (August 20th). The company obtains UNI EN ISO 14001 certification for its environmental management system. This gives rise to a comprehensive project for the protection of the environment and resources that is formalized in 2009 as Scavolini Green Mind. The Crystal kitchen (Studio Vuesse) is introduced. Still today one of the company's premiere models, it is innovative for the use of glass doors and exposed surfaces. The Group's revenues exceed 180 million euros. Studio Roscio, a PR agency in Milan, begins collaborating with Scavolini.

Emanuela Scavolini
My father Elvino? His imposing build barely hid the inner identity of a gentle and playful man who loved spending time with children and planting flowers in the garden surrounding our home. We all remember him with great tenderness. He had the strong hands of a laborer, "hands of gold", as his mother, my grandmother Teresa used to call them. He was a true child of the sharecropping culture that was quite widespread in our region, and as such he knew how to do a bit of everything— gardening, his real specialty, carpentry, plumbing, painting…. He embodied all the qualities of the artisan, a figure that is now seen in a very positive light. But despite all his success in business, he was a truly simple and shy man who loved family life and avoided public and social events whenever possible. He was passionate about food, a gourmet in fact, and my mother always took great care in preparing all the vegetables that he would grow. He remained loyal to himself for his entire life, and his closest friends were always the same ones he had known as child in his hometown of San Veneranda, where he always felt at home at the local social club, where he and my mother had celebrated their wedding reception. After his death, we were inundated with expressions of affection from

The Scavolini canteen
in Montelabbate, 2010
Photo Filippo Romano

people we didn't even know, people whom he had helped in times of need. Moving letters, like the one from a woman from Fano who had received help from my father without ever knowing him directly. But she had not forgotten. In the end, these are the things that remind me and my siblings what a great father we had, a father who guided us with few words and much affection through our lives and careers. The same affection—along with mutual respect—that characterized his relationship with Valter. They got along harmoniously their whole lives, sharing their work duties in accordance with their natures: Uncle Valter the commercial guy, my father the production guy. It's touching now to think back to his innate modesty, through which he considered himself more a carpenter than a businessman. If I had to fit myself into all of this, I would say that I'm a 'straddler', insofar as I'm the first-born, straddling the line between the old and the new generation. This means that when I think about the early years of our company, I can say in a certain sense that I was there to experience them, though through the eyes of a child, of course. I remember the many people who worked for us and who are now in retirement: Renato, Feliciano, Orlando, Giuliano, Nerina, Iole, Giuseppe, Ferdinando, Elvidio, Astorre, Luciano, Donatella, Alberto…a long list of names and faces still dear to me. Like Maria, the company's first secretary, who worked out of an office in our house. My father would sometimes take me with him to the plant, and I remember the kindness of the workers, particularly Romolo and Vittorio, who used to let me help them—or at least they made me think so—to plate the honeycomb panels. Then there were the lunches for San Giuseppe, protector of carpenters, which were very important to my

father; it was a sacred ritual and everyone had to attend, an opportunity to be together around a table. I began working in the company in 1980. My father had convinced me to try it for a while, leaving me free to decide if I wanted to stay. I instantly fell in love with the work, the overall atmosphere and above all the people. Many of my colleagues from back then are still with me today, and I've always felt that I was lucky to have grown up alongside them. Our tutor was the legendary '*Ragioniere*', as he was known to all— adding the name Nobili was superfluous. After a time in sales, where I had the chance to understand the various phases of production, I began concentrating on human resources. The climate of today, with 660 employees, has certainly changed a bit, and I must admit that it's sometimes hard for me to remember each one's name. But one thing hasn't changed, and that is that we still work as a team. Naturally we're more organized today, but we still see the work of every single employee as important, indeed fundamental. At Scavolini, everyone matters. Even a tiny error can cause problems for colleagues and for the final user. Our company looks to the future, which is why we invest in young people. In fact, 30% of our workforce is under 30. We believe it is our duty to help young people in their professional growth, which is why every new hire is assigned to a tutor, much like Nobili was for me. Then we meet with various department heads to evaluate the progress of each new employee. This is the most gratifying part of my job, seeing in those young people the same enthusiasm I felt when I was their age, just starting out at Scavolini, believing in them, guiding them. Every now and then I'm asked to recount how this company was born and how it

Above
Expositive totem Scavolini
De-Sign Lab, 2006

Below
Graphical introduction to
Scavolini Green Mind,
2009

developed, and when I do I try to communicate the values on which Scavolini is founded—the same values I try to pass on to my own children. *Director of Public Relations and Human Resources for Scavolini; President of the Fondazione Scavolini*

2005

After a period of suspension, Scavolini returns to the SAMP trade show in Pesaro, presenting the two new flagship models, Crystal and Glam (the latter designed by Marco Pareschi). In collaboration with the Marche branch of ADI (Industrial Design Association), Scavolini De-Sign Lab is created and the first Scavolini Kitchens Workshop is held, with the aim of discovering new expressive and functional avenues in the field of kitchen design. Of the twenty or so young Italian and foreign designers participating in the workshop, three projects are chosen, with first prize going to Dual by Robin Rizzino. The initiative is presented at the Milan Triennial exhibition on June 28th, 2006.

2006

Scavolini adopts an advanced planning and management system (SAP) designed to optimize the production chain and rationalize the order schedule with the products coming off the line, all built to order, eliminating downtime and storage costs. Historic development

in sales strategy with the opening of the first Scavolini Stores in Bari and Verona, instantly recognizable mono-brand showrooms intended to support the existing distribution network. During the 16th Eurocucina in Milan, Scavolini presents Flux (which entered the catalogue the following year), a model by Giugiaro Design that combines technology with the new line of formal enquiry undertaken by the brand. "Our approach to this project," explains Fabrizio Giugiaro, "was to combine the client's desire to develop an innovative kitchen concept with the modularity of an industrial product. So we started with the idea of curved, dynamic shaping for all the storage elements, which is then emphasized by the contrast with the more austere and linear forms of the appliances. This led to the adoption of a system of drawers for the lower cabinets and transom doors for the upper cupboards, thus making the system more ergonomic. Once the initial layout of the modules was established, we worked in two different but complementary directions, conjugating the new concept in a hi-tech version and a more essential version." The Baccarat model (Absolute Classic collection) is completely different. Presented at the same trade show with Flux, this kitchen relaunches Scavolini products aimed at a clientele, which has been present all along, that wants a more traditional kitchen. In the words

CI VUOLE UNA MENTE VERDE PER IMMAGINARE UN MONDO MIGLIORE.

A certificate of excellence used by Scavolini sales points, 2009

of designer Gianni Pareschi, "the classicism of a product is not measured by its number of stylistic signifiers, but by its capacity to revive the essence of an important cultural heritage."

2007

Revenues for the Scavolini Group surpass 230 million euros. The company continues to grow in Italy and abroad.

2008

November marks the start of the operation for *Kitchens.it*, transformed for the occasion into *Kitchens Daily*—an unprecedented launch in the Italian print media that involves 35 local and national daily newspapers for approximately three weeks. In December Scavolini obtains OHSAS 18001 certification for its health and safety management program for the workplace, the first kitchen manufacturer in Italy to do so. The integration of Scavolini's three certified systems (quality, environment, health and safety, verified by SGS Italia, an independent organization for the certification of industrial goods and services) allows the company to significantly improve shared activities and services, streamlining the

procedures and optimizing timeframes. This synergy leads to the pursuit of the 'continuous improvement' that constitutes the primary objective required by international norms and by Scavolini's own policy. Robursport Scavolini Pesaro wins its first league title in women's volleyball. Raffaello Pravato premieres Amélie at the 2007 edition of SAMP in Pesaro, a model that reinterprets traditional forms using natural materials in a reliable and durable way. The idea of the kitchen as a sort of theatrical stage is captured by Scenery, presented in Milan at the 17th Eurocucina. It is a 'transversal' design, with a powerful communicative and aesthetic impact. Designers Perry King and Santiago Miranda, working for the first time in the kitchen sector, demonstrate careful reflection in both cultural and technical terms: "The kitchen has become the center of social life for the family, the locus of encounter and interaction. It is gradually invading the living area and incorporating many of its functions— the person cooking wants to participate in the family communication; the guest doesn't want to be left alone by the cook. The broad openness of Scenery responds to this need for participation

In-house information
brochures, 2007, 2009
and 2010

and socialization, but it also resolves the problems—the inevitable mess, the abrupt shifts in temperature and humidity, the odors—that normal mortals generate when we cook." The Milan trade show also features other new products that would enter the catalogue the following year. Karim Rashid interprets the vitreous skin of Crystal with his stylized graphics: "Decoration for me is a way to communicate, to give depth and dynamism to the objects that animate our space, pushing the eye past the surface of things." Cultural eclecticism and attention to the tactile qualities of materials, which are treated to give a rust effect (for the bronzed metal components) or a light-absorbing opacity (for the granite panels) are the distinguishing features of the

Tribe kitchen by Marcello Cutino – BCF design: "It is the discovery of new perceptual possibilities that introduce innovative features to the space of the kitchen. A project rich in the sensations of color, surface and form."

2009

Scavolini reinforces its communications in the print media with the supplement *Kitchens.it*. As a signal of optimism in reaction to the international economic crisis, the print run is doubled from 4 to 8 million copies. Confirming its commitment to the region and to environmental and socio-cultural issues, the company launches Scavolini Green Mind, a program that focuses on ecosustainability: Scavolini commits to using ecological materials for all its panels, with a minimum emission of

Meeting with the Scavolini resellers at the SAMP, Pesaro 2007

formaldehyde, and to using only energy from renewable sources meeting the standards Impatto Zero®. Thanks to an agreement with LifeGate, all CO2 emissions relating to the supply of electrical energy are compensated by the creation and upkeep of more than 21 acres of forested areas in Italy and Costa Rica. Scavolini participates in several important international trade shows and expands its network of foreign sales points, from England (new store in Wokingham, Berkshire, one of the wealthiest parts of southern England) to Belgium to India, in preparation for a capillary intercontinental expansion that has begun to involve Africa in significant measure. The new campaign "You can always expect the best from a Scavolini kitchen" is launched in September. In December, the new Scavolini Store Milano in Viale Enrico Martini is opened, the 41st such store and the largest in Italy, with 8,400 square feet of display area. Robursport Scavolini Pesaro wins its second league title.

2010

Working from experience accumulated over 15 years (since the "Growing Together" program of 1994), Scavolini

Academy begins offering an e-learning service on the company extranet platform to its dealers. A new campaign is undertaken in March for *Kitchens.it* in about 40 Italian newspapers, this time reaching 20 million copies. Scavolini continues sponsoring the Pesaro women's volleyball team, which wins its third consecutive title, and co-sponsoring the men's basketball team. The Rossini Opera Festival celebrates its 30th anniversary, with Scavolini constantly by its side since 1982. In Milan, at the 18th Eurocucina show, the Scavolini stand presents flagship products and new models with the slogan "Experience the red. Taste more." Among the new products are Tetrix (Michael Young), Attitùde (Lorella Agnoletto and Stefano Spessotto), inspired by the world of Italian fashion, and Regard (Raffaello Pravato), a hybrid version of the classical and the modern. A new entry in the catalogue is Atelier (Studio Vuesse), an austere and elegant kitchen that is "free of schemes, easy to configure".

2011

Tetrix, designed by Michael Young, goes into production.

The Robursport women's volleyball team of Pesaro, several times champions of Italy, 2010

Valter Scavolini

Now that we've reached the end of this long and, for me, exciting chronology of significant events, a sort of diary of our first fifty years of activity, I would like to add a few reflections of my own. Nothing self-glorifying, don't worry, I'm not the type. Just a few scattered notes and thoughts. When I think back to the beginning, sure, the work was hard, as much as 20 hours a day, but it didn't weigh on me. The hours flew by. Starting up a business was a dream that was coming true. I'd had to twist my father's arm a bit for his help—after all, when I started the company I was only 19. Nowadays, people are still children at that age, but we were the postwar generation, we knew how to roll up our sleeves and push ourselves. I was absolutely convinced that we could do it. I never had any doubt. Things went well because we knew enough to always plan important decisions in advance. I think this rule applies to life as well. One should never wait until things turn sour to find the energy to react, one must always anticipate, always have a clear idea today of what you'll need to do tomorrow, the day after, or better still, next year. With this approach, which I have to say we have always applied with absolute consistency, the difficult periods for the company have been rather limited, in a certain sense we never experienced any at all. And we weren't born yesterday, we have 50 years of work under our belts. I think that the necessary traits for running a large company are different and many, but I maintain that in some way a person has to be born with the makings of a businessman. It's an extremely difficult profession, occupying your entire life and never leaving you a moment's rest. Of course it's also fascinating, a consuming passion. But it's not as though that's all I think

about. I have a big, beautiful family and a passion for sport. Any chance I get I'll jump on a bicycle or go running, play tennis, swim. In the winter, whenever I can get 'permission' for a couple of days off from work, I go skiing. I'm also an avid gardener. I have my own vegetable garden on the hill next to our factory. Examining myself, I have to say that my family history had a significant impact on me, for it was there that I absorbed the basic notions that would serve me for the rest of my life. Before going into business, my parents were farmers, and being a farmer means to a certain degree being in business. My family grew wheat and vegetables, and they had some dairy cows. Their work in the fields was supplemented by their work at the market in Pesaro, where they sold what they grew. I, who used to help them along with my brother, learned a lot from them about daily commitment and constancy, the ABCs of planning. It's not as though one can become a farmer from one day to the next. If you make mistakes one season, the next year you're broke, finished. Knowing the details of one's profession, knowing them well, is another fundamental requirement. This means that you always have to be up to date, dialoguing every day with those around you and beside you, with managers, technicians, laborers. My hands-on involvement nowadays is necessarily limited, but I spent years working side by side with the production staff. I've always had a direct relationship with our employees, I grew up with them. Another important factor is that we're truly rooted in the Pesaro community, where almost all our employees come from. Trusting others, relying on the people who are close to you is necessary for moving forward and growing together. The aspects that make me proudest about the whole Scavolini adventure are

the size and importance that we have achieved. Being at the top of the Italian market since 1984 is clearly a source of pride for me. But I'm also proud that neither I nor any of us have ever let it go to our heads. Rather than resting on the laurels of past glory, we have always looked ahead. Now our field of action is the world market, and we want to continue moving ahead in it. In this new international scenario, we are and always will be an Italian brand, one that produces in Italy and relies on a chain of suppliers who are and must remain Italian. I've said this many times, to my fellow businessmen and on official occasions: I am firmly convinced that all industrial initiatives that strive to maintain and develop jobs in our country should be supported. It's too easy to fly the 'Made in Italy' banner and then go produce your goods elsewhere. I see enormous risk in that for our company. In today's globalized market, quality still pays, believe me. For us, quality means guaranteeing our clients all over the world that Scavolini is 100% Italian, and so it shall remain.

Founder and President, Scavolini

Filippo Romano

Montelabbate, Pesaro
July 2010

pp. 164–5
Valter Scavolini

p. 166
Gian Marco, Emanuela,
Valter, Fabiana and
Alberto Scavolini

p. 167
Alberto and Emanuela
Scavolini

p. 168
Gian Marco and Fabiana
Scavolini

p. 169
Vittorio Renzi

Scavolini Kitchens 1962–2011

Massimo Martignoni

The following registry lists all the models ever produced in chronological order (determined by the year a given model went into production), with the name of the designer/s and any special program or collection to which it may belong. Dates framed by parentheses indicate the year the entry model was designed, in the event that it differs from the date of production. At the end are the models that remain in the prototype phase

1962

Svedese
Studio Vuesse

1963

Finest
Studio Vuesse

Italia
Studio Vuesse

1967

Flower
Studio Vuesse

1968

Uraki
Studio Vuesse

1969

Color
Studio Vuesse

1975

Connye
Agostino Bertani

L'isola della Melarosa
Agostino Bertani

1976

Harmony
Studio Vuesse

Selquy
Studio Vuesse

1978

Happy
Dante Benini

L'Elite
Simone Donato

Merry
Dante Benini

1979

Cardya
Studio Vuesse

Every
Studio Vuesse

Sanya
Studio Vuesse

1980

Easy
Simone Donato

Lucciola
Agostino Bertani

Pitty
Simone Donato

1981

Lady
Agostino and Ave Bertani

1982

Fanny
Simone Donato

Melody
Studio Vuesse

Trapezio
Enrico Tonucci

1983

Ambrarosa
Agostino Bertani

Cabriolet
Pierluigi Molinari

Dolly
Studio Vuesse

Fiordaliso
Studio Vuesse

Lovely (1982)
Studio Vuesse

Meridiana
Studio Vuesse

1984

Emily
Studio Vuesse

Gardenia
Studio Vuesse

Raffaella (1983)
Studio Vuesse

1985

Arianna
Studio Vuesse

Dolly Family
Studio Vuesse

Isabel
Studio Vuesse

1986

Angelica
Studio Vuesse

Camelia
Studio Vuesse

Dandy (1985)
Studio Vuesse

Fairy (1985)
Studio Vuesse

Jenny (1985)
Studio Vuesse

Ketty (1985)
Studio Vuesse

1988

Donna Rosa (1987)
Roberto Ciolli

Lorella (1987)
Silvano Barsacchi

Milady
Roberto Ciolli

1989

Alison
Silvano Barsacchi

Honey (1988)
Silvano Barsacchi

Lucilla
Studio Vuesse

1990

Melania
Roberto Ciolli

Meryl (1988)
Studio Vuesse

Blondie
Silvano Barsacchi

Lietta
Silvano Barsacchi

Melissa (1989)
Roberto Ciolli

1991   **1992**

Ortensia
Roberto Ciolli

Arabella
Studio Vuesse

Fiandra (1990)
Silvano Barsacchi

Altea (1991)
Studio Vuesse

Arlette
Studio Vuesse

Gemma (1990)
Jonathan De Pas, Donato D'Urbino,
Paolo Lomazzi

Ambra (1991)
Silvano Barsacchi

Beatrice
Roberto Ciolli

Mimsy (1990)
Roberto Lucci, Paolo Orlandini

Malva (1991)
Roberto Ciolli

1993

Novella (1991)
Studio Vuesse

Petunia (1991)
Giuliano Cappelletti, Enzo Pozzoli

Begonia
Roberto Ciolli

Country (1991)
Gianni Pareschi

Flora (1992)
Silvano Barsacchi

Mirta (1992)
Roberto Ciolli

Vanilla (1992)
Studio Vuesse

Verbena (1992)
Gianni Pareschi

1994

Dalia (1993)
Giuliano Cappelletti, Enzo Pozzoli

Gilia (1993)
Giuliano Cappelletti, Enzo Pozzoli

Jasmine (1993)
Roberto Ciolli

1995

Oxalis
Silvano Barsacchi

Charme (1994)
Roberto Ciolli

Glory
Roberto Ciolli

Pepita
Silvano Barsacchi

Silene (1993)
Roberto Ciolli

Garden
Roberto Ciolli

Love
Studio Vuesse

Regia (1994)
Studio Castiglia

Valeriana (1993)
Roberto Ciolli

Glady
Studio Vuesse

Ninfea (1994)
Studio Vuesse

1996

1997

Domobel (1995)
Raffaello Pravato

Maranta (1995)
Roberto Ciolli

Alma (1996)
Studio Flamek

Rosel (1996)
Studio Flamek

Edenia (1995)
Silvano Barsacchi

Fiamma
Silvano Barsacchi

Farm (1995)
Gianni Pareschi

Galatea (1996)
Raffaello Pravato

1998

1999

Gala (1997)
Silvano Barsacchi

Vetta
Studio Flamek

Baltimora (1998)
Studio Vuesse with Marco Pareschi

Tess (1998)
Silvano Barsacchi

Madison (1997)
Silvano Barsacchi

Carol (1998)
Studio Vuesse

Sonia
Studio Flamek

Darling (1998)
Raffaello Pravato

2000

2001

Alis (1999)
Studio Vuesse

Melville (1999)
Silvano Barsacchi

Astra (1999)
Silvano Barsacchi

Margot (2000)
Studio Vuesse

Flo' (1999)
Studio Vuesse

Susan (1999)
Studio Vuesse

Cometa (1999)
Silvano Barsacchi

Megan (2000)
Studio Vuesse

Maryland (1999)
Studio Vuesse

Corinne (1999)
Raffaello Pravato

Vega (1999)
Silvano Barsacchi

2002

2003

Avellana (2000)
Raffaello Pravato

Adria
Studio Vuesse

City (2002)
Studio Vuesse
Happening Program

Home (2002)
Studio Vuesse
Happening Program

Malaga (2000)
Raffaello Pravato

Aliante (2000)
Studio Vuesse

Dream (2002)
Studio Vuesse
Happening Program

Life (2002)
Studio Vuesse
Happening Program

Utility System
Renzo Baldanello, Bernardino Pittino

Brio
Studio Vuesse

Duetto
Studio Vuesse

Play (2002)
Studio Vuesse
Happening Program

2004

Zeffiro (2000)
Studio Vuesse

Belvedere (2003)
Raffaello Pravato

Cora (2003)
Raffaello Pravato

Crystal (2003)
Studio Vuesse

2005

Glam (2004)
Marco Pareschi

2006

Madeleine (2005)
Studio Vuesse

Mood (2005)
Silvano Barsacchi

Sax (2005)
Studio Vuesse

2007

Flux (2006)
Giugiaro Design

Rainbow (2006)
Studio Vuesse
Happening Program

Reflex (2006)
Marco Pareschi

2008

Amélie (2007)
Raffaello Pravato

Baccarat (2006)
Gianni Pareschi & Co.
Absolute Classic Collection

Focus (2006)
Gianni Pareschi & Co.

Grand Relais
Gianni Pareschi & Co.
Absolute Classic Collection

Long Island
Gianni Pareschi & Co.
Absolute Classic Collection

Scenery (2006)
Perry King, Santiago Miranda

2009

**Crystal Texture
by Karim Rashid (2008)**
Karim Rashid

Flirt (2008)
Studio Vuesse

Tribe (2006)
Marcello Cutino

2010

Atelier (2009)
Studio Vuesse

Esprit (2009)
Studio Vuesse

Regard (2009)
Raffaello Pravato

2011

Tetrix (2010)
Michael Young

Models not in production

1973
Oliena
Studio Vuesse

1974
Luana
Studio Vuesse

1975
Play
Studio Vuesse

1976
Greta
Studio Vuesse

1991
Desire'
Roberto Ciolli

1993
Artemisia
Studio Vuesse
Clivia
Idea Institute
Corolla
Agostino Bertani
Genziana
Studio Vuesse
Ribes
Idea Institute

1994
Inga
Studio Vuesse
Meta
Giuliano Cappelletti, Enzo Pozzoli

1996
Aura
Giuliano Cappelletti, Enzo Pozzoli
Loira
Studio Vuesse
Maya
Studio Vuesse

1998
Isadora
Raffaello Pravato

2000
Alice
Giuliano Cappelletti, Enzo Pozzoli
Bistrot
Gianni Pareschi
Clea
Raffaello Pravato
Morgana
Raffaello Pravato

2002
Fly
Studio Vuesse

Bibliography

Valentina Dalla Costa

The list contains only titles of the most important company publications

Scavolini cucine componibili, Effegi, Florence, corporate publication, 1982.

Scavolini [monograph celebrating 20 years of history], company monograph, Muzzio, Padova, corporate publication, 1983.

La cucina più amata dagli italiani, corporate publication, 1984.

Scavolini accessori, Muzzio, Padova, corporate publication, 1986.

Una nuova campagna pubblicitaria della Scavolini Spa con la gioia di vivere di Lorella Cuccarini, corporate publication, 1987.

La nuova campagna pubblicitaria della Scavolini. La cucina come emozione, corporate publication, 1989.

Moderno italiano. Nascita ed evoluzione dell'industria mobiliera pesarese, G. Morpurgo (ed.), Fondazione Scavolini, Franco Cosimo Panini, Modena 1990.

Manuale di identificazione grafica Scavolini, corporate publication, 1991.

R. Martufi, "Vediamoci in villa. Le vicende di villa Montani di Ginestreto, sede di rappresentanza dell'azienda e sede della Fondazione Scavolini", in *Pesaro Open*, June 1991.

Scavolini. Campagna pubblicitaria 1992, corporate publication, 1992.

1962-1992. Trent'anni di cucine Scavolini, edited by Scavolini's public relations office, O.G.M., Padova, corporate publication, 1993.

Scavolini. Campagna pubblicitaria, Ramberti, Rimini, corporate publication, 1994.

L'arredo giusto per le nostre cucine, corporate publication, 1996.

S. Balduini, *Un modello di comunicazione integrata: la "Scavolini" cucine, 1984-1994*, degree thesis, Università degli studi di Urbino, Department of Literature and Philosophy, 1995-96.

Scavolini. Campagna promopubblicitaria, corporate publication, 1996.

Il mobile pesarese. Dai maestri artigiani alla produzione industriale, G. Calegari, P. Giannotti (eds.), Fondazione Cassa di Risparmio di Pesaro, Il lavoro editoriale, Ancona 2000.

"Kitchens.it", annual corporate publication, 2001-2008, biannual (come "Kitchens by Scavolini") from 2009.

Io tengo per Scavolini. I nuovi linguaggi per la campagna di una grande marca, corporate publication, 2002.

F. Andreani, *Scavolini: la strategia fa la costruzione della marca*, diploma thesis, Università degli studi di Urbino, Department of Economics, 2002-2003.

Monografia Scavolini [celebrating 40 years of history], edited by Studio Komma, corporate publication, 2003.

A. Masucci, "Valter Scavolini. Da 21 anni in cucina comando io", in *Corriere Dossier*, supplement to *Corriere della Sera*, March 3rd, 2005.

M. Pillinini, "Una di famiglia", in *Spazio Casa*, June 2005.

P. Guidi, "Una cucina 'rosso Ferrari'", in *Il Sole24 Ore*, April 7th, 2006.

A. Montalbetti, "Vent'anni in vetta alle classifiche", in *Built In*, June 2006.

A. Galdo, "Metto il lusso sul fuoco", in *Panorama Economy*, August 9th, 2006.

"I vincitori del 1° Scavolini kitchens workshop", in *GdA - Il Giornale dell'Arredamento*, September 2006.

"Valter Scavolini", in *Ambiente Cucina*, October 31st, 2006.

C. Cavaliere, R. Razzano, "Un grande marchio e venti designer", in *Ambiente Cucina*, October 2006.

R. Linguini, "Scavolini, è amore da più di vent'anni", in *Gente*, April 5th, 2007.

"Per una cucina accessibile a tutti", in *DDN Cucine*, September 2007.

A. Magistà, "Finalmente in cucina c'è tutto lo spazio per cucinare", in *Il Venerdì di Repubblica*, April 11th, 2008.

"Scavolini pensa all'estero", in *Pambianco Week*, April 14th, 2008.

"Scavolini Store, l'acquisto diventa esperienza", in *Built In*, April 2008.

"Scavolini, the Italian kitchen loved by the world", in *Ambiente Cucina*, September 2008.

"Scavolini, massimo storico di fatturato", in *CorrierEconomia*, supplement to *Corriere della Sera*, October 20th, 2008.

L. Wildermuth, "Scavolini, le cucine senza crisi", in *Affari & Finanza*, supplement to *La Repubblica*, November 3rd, 2008.

L. Gualtieri, "Scavolini, valanga di spot anticrisi", in *MF*, November 26th, 2008.

M. Zio, "Le cucine Scavolini alla conquista dell'India", in *MF fashion*, December 2nd, 2008.

C. Benna, "Scavolini, la cucina diventa 'verde'", in *Affari & Finanza*, supplement to *La Repubblica*, December 14th, 2009.

D. Panosetti, "Un patto condiviso per l'impresa-famiglia", in *Dossier*, supplement to *Il Giornale*, January 1st, 2009.

"Nasce Scavolini Green Mind", in *Pambianco Week*, February 5th, 2009.

"Nasce Scavolini Green Mind", in *Hachette Home Italia*, February 2009.

"Ecosostenibilità con Scavolini Green Mind", in *CorrierEconomia*, supplement to *Corriere della Sera*, March 2nd, 2009.

R. Carbutti, "La cucina del futuro? Tecnologica e soprattutto sarà intelligente", in *Il Giorno*, March 2nd, 2009.

"Scavolini, Kitchen goes green... nasce Scavolini Green Mind: il nuovo progetto di Scavolini per un nuovo modo di fare impresa all'insegna dell'eco sostenibilità", in *La Repubblica*, March 15th, 2009.

A. Bersani, "L'Italia che vince", in *Panorama*, May 28th, 2009.

B. Gerosa, "Pensare in verde", in *Brava Casa*, May 2009.

"Un valore costruito ogni giorno", in *Dossier Marche*, supplement to *Il Giornale*, June 17th, 2009.

"Scavolini Green Mind", in *Casabella*, June 2009.

T. Potenza, "Voglio il mondo dietro le mie cucine", in *Panorama Economy*, July 29th, 2009.

A. Rocca, " Scavolini presenta la sua nuova campagna multimediale ideata da Komma. Budget 2009 a 15 mln.", in *Daily Media*, September 17th, 2009.

M. Pillinini, "Pionieri del made in Italy", in *Spazio Casa*, October 2009.

"Cucina grandi scelte", in *Casamica*, November 14th, 2009.

"Scavolini Green Mind: studi e progetti per 'fare impresa' in modo sostenibile", in *Corriere della Sera*, November 30th, 2009.

M. Modafferi, "Scavolini sfida la crisi. Investendo", in *Italia Oggi*, December 18th, 2009.

"Scavolini Store Milano: 1000mq di design e qualità", in *Il Giorno*, December 19th, 2009.

C. Viglino, *Scavolini*, in *Tendenze, progetto, prodotto. Una ricerca sulla filiera del furniture design*, G. Bersano (ed.), Editrice Compositori, Bologna 2009.

E. Comelli, "Scavolini, cucina con vista su Manhattan", in *CorrierEconomia*, supplement to *Corriere della Sera*, January 11th, 2010.

"Scavolini: qualità e innovazione", in *Corriere della Sera*, January 24th, 2010.

R. Ciuffa, "Valter Scavolini: la mia è la cucina più amata dagli italiani", in *Specchio Economico*, January 2010.

A. Martinelli, "La cucina in testa", in *Interni Panorama*, January 2010.

T. Villa, "L'importanza di chiamarsi Ernesto", in *Case da Abitare*, January 2010.

"Scavolini si aggiudica il Merit Award. Qualità e innovazione non solo in cucina", in *Il Mondo*, February 12th, 2010.

F. Mannoni, "Scavolini azzera le emissioni di CO2", in *Il Sole 24 Ore*, March 3rd, 2010.

M. Gennari, "La crisi non si subisce, s'affronta", in *Il Resto del Carlino*, March 16th, 2010.

C. De Cesare, "Cucina tra due fuochi", in *Corriere Design*, supplement to *Corriere della Sera*, April 13th, 2010.

"Scavolini taglia i consumi e studia i clienti sul web", in *Panorama*, April 2010.

F. Vincenzi, "Crescere in cucina", in *Dossier Marche*, in *Il Mondo*, June 25th, 2010.

"Le ragioni di un successo", in *Ambiente Cucina*, June 2010

Index of Names